GET BY IN FRENCH

A QUICK BEGINNER'S COURSE FOR HOLIDAYMAKERS AND BUSINESS PEOPLE

PIERRICK PICOT

Published by BBC Books
a division of BBC Enterprises Ltd
Woodlands
80 Wood Lane
London W12 0TT

First published 1992
Reprinted 1992 (three times)
Reprinted 1993, 1994

Edited by Iris Sprankling
General Editor: Alan Wilding

ISBN 0 563 36130 1

Designed by Peter Bridgewater
Map and illustrations by Lorraine Harrison
Cover illustration by Tony Masero

Set in Great Britain by
Central Southern Typesetters, Eastbourne
Printed and bound in Great Britain by Clays Ltd, St Ives plc

Cover printed by Clays Ltd, St Ives plc

Exclusive U.S. Distributor of the Get By in Series Packs

Ambrose Video Publishing, Inc.
1290 Avenue of the Americas
Suite 2245
New York,
N.Y. 10104

CONTENTS

CALAIS
LILLE
BOULOGNE
DIEPPE
CHERBOURG
ROUEN
SEINE
REIMS
NANCY
STRASBOURG
PARIS
MARNE
NORMANDIE
CHARTRES
BREST
RENNES
BRETAGNE
LES VASGES
ALSACE
ANGERS
TOURS
DIJON
SAÔNE
QUIMPER
LOIRE
BEAUNE
NANTES
BOURGES
POITIERS
BOURGOGNE
LES ALPES
CLERMONT FERRAND
RHÔNE
LYON
PERIGUEUX
DORDOGNE
GRENOBLE
BORDEAUX
PROVENCE
GARONNE
AVIGNON
AIX-EN-PROVENCE
TOULOUSE
LES PYRENEES
MONTPELLIER
MARSEILLE
CANNES

INTRODUCTION

The new BBC *Get by in French* is a six-unit course for anyone planning a visit to a French-speaking country. It provides a basic 'survival kit' for some of the situations you're likely to find yourself in.

Get by in French is especially designed for those who have little or no knowledge of French, so that they can get more enjoyment out of their trips abroad. The course consists of two audiocassettes and this book.

The *audiocassettes* concentrate on what you'll need to say and understand to cope with a particular situation – getting something to eat and drink, finding somewhere to stay, asking the way, for example. They include real-life conversations recorded in France, to let you hear everyday French right from the start and they also give you opportunities to repeat words and phrases you hear in the conversations and to work out for yourself how to 'get by'.

All the recordings were made during Marie-Pierre's visit to Angers in the west of France. Angers is situated on the river Maine, 90 minutes away from Paris by TGV (train à grande vitesse), France's high-speed train. Gateway to the châteaux of the Loire Valley, Angers is an elegant and pleasant town to visit with its pedestrian streets, gardens and parks.

The *Get by* book is divided into six sections, each comprising six parts:

- the main key words and expressions you'll need to follow the recorded conversations.
- the texts of the recorded conversations.
- additional words and phrases you've come across in the conversations.
- some explanations on the language used.
- exercises, for you to practise what you've learnt.

- some information you may find useful while in France.

At the back of the book, you'll find a useful Reference section including, for example, a list of numbers, the key to the exercises and a French-English vocabulary list.

TO MAKE THE MOST OF THE COURSE

- Start by reading the key words and expressions.
- Listen carefully to the cassette, joining in the activities and exercises as you go along. It's best not to read the printed conversations the first time round so that you can see how much you can understand without them. Play the same conversation as many times as you like. Use the additional words and phrases if you need to.
- Then read the explanations.
- Finally, try out what you've been learning in the exercises. Keys are at the back of the book.

It's a good idea, if you can, to work through the exercises with someone else. You'll also have plenty of opportunities to practise your pronunciation using the cassette. At the end of the cassette is a recording of all the words in the Pronunciation Guide at the back of this book, with pauses for you to repeat them.

Good luck with your French . . . *Bon courage!*

1 MEETING PEOPLE & ORDERING DRINKS

KEY WORDS AND PHRASES

bonjour	good morning, good afternoon
bonsoir	good evening, good night
au revoir	goodbye
Comment allez-vous?	How are you?
Ça va?	How are things?
Ça va!	Fine!
Vous êtes d'Angers?	Are you from Angers?
Vous êtes d'où?	Where are you from?
je suis de Lille	I'm from Lille
s'il vous plaît	please
merci	thank you
un thé, s'il vous plaît	a tea, please
deux bières, s'il vous plaît	two beers, please
pour moi, un martini	a martini for me

CONVERSATIONS

HELLO, HOW ARE THINGS?

ANNE	Bonjour, Marie-Noël.
MARIE-NOEL	Bonjour, Anne.
ANNE	Ça va?
MARIE-NOEL	Ça va. Et vous?
ANNE	Très bien, merci.

GOOD MORNING, HOW ARE YOU?

M. DOREAU	Bonjour, Monsieur Bouillon. Comment allez-vous?
M. BOUILLON	Très bien, je vous remercie. Et vous-même?
M. DOREAU	Ça va très bien.

GOOD EVENING

BEATRICE	Oh, bonsoir.
PIERRICK	Bonsoir, Béatrice. Voici Marie-Pierre.
BEATRICE	Bonsoir, Marie-Pierre.
MARIE-PIERRE	Bonsoir, Béatrice.

GOODBYE, THANK YOU VERY MUCH

MARIE-PIERRE	Au revoir, madame, et merci beaucoup.
MME HOPPELER	Au revoir, madame.
PIERRICK	Au revoir, madame.
MME HOPPELER	Au revoir, monsieur.
PIERRICK	Merci.

ARE YOU FROM ANGERS?

MARIE-PIERRE	Béatrice, vous êtes d'Angers?
BEATRICE	Non, je suis de Lille.

WHERE ARE YOU FROM?

MARIE-PIERRE	Monsieur Michaud, vous êtes d'Angers?
M. MICHAUD	Non, je ne suis pas d'Angers.
MARIE-PIERRE	Vous êtes d'où alors?
M. MICHAUD	Je suis d'Avignon.

I'M ENGLISH

MARIE-PIERRE	Vous n'êtes pas française?
BARBARA	Non, non. Je suis anglaise.
MARIE-PIERRE	Ah, vous êtes anglaise! Et vous êtes d'où?
BARBARA	Je suis de Chichester.

BREAKFAST

SERVEUSE	Bonjour.
MARIE-PIERRE	Bonjour.
SERVEUSE	Vous désirez? Café, thé ou chocolat?
MARIE-PIERRE	Chocolat, s'il vous plaît.
SERVEUSE	D'accord. Je vous sers tout de suite.

AT THE *PATISSERIE*

MME GABORIEAU	Que désirez-vous, monsieur-dame?
PIERRICK	Deux thés, s'il vous plaît.
MME GABORIEAU	Oui. Nature, lait, citron?
MARIE-PIERRE	Un thé au lait, s'il vous plaît.
MME GABORIEAU	Oui. Et pour monsieur?
PIERRICK	Au citron, s'il vous plaît.
MME GABORIEAU	Oui.

ORDERING DRINKS

PIERRICK	S'il vous plaît.
M. MENARD	Bonsoir, messieurs-dame. Que désirez-vous boire?
PIERRICK	Marie-Pierre?
MARIE-PIERRE	Un citron pressé pour moi, s'il vous plaît.
PIERRICK	Et deux bières, s'il vous plaît.
M. MENARD	Deux bières? Bouteille ou pression?
PIERRICK	Pour vous Didier?
DIDIER	Bouteille, s'il vous plaît.
PIERRICK	Et pour moi pression.
M. MENARD	Bien sûr.

AN APERITIF?

BEATRICE	Vous voulez un apéritif?
PIERRICK	Oui, merci. Oui.
MARIE-PIERRE	Oui, merci.
BEATRICE	Du martini, du whisky, du porto, du jus d'orange?

MARIE-PIERRE	Pour moi un martini, s'il vous plaît.
BEATRICE	Et Pierrick?
PIERRICK	Et moi un whisky.
BEATRICE	D'accord.

CHEERS!

PIERRICK	Tchin, tchin!
MARIE-PIERRE	Tchin, tchin!
BEATRICE	Tchin!
PIERRICK	A la vôtre!
BEATRICE	A la vôtre!

NUMBERS

PIERRICK	Tu sais compter jusqu'à dix?
FABIEN	Oui.
PIERRICK	Vas-y.
FABIEN	Un, deux, trois, quatre, cinq, six, sept, huit, neuf, dix.
PIERRICK	Allez. Vas-y encore. Lentement.
FABIEN	Un, deux, trois, quatre, cinq, six, sept, huit, neuf, dix.
PIERRICK	Très bien!

WORD LIST

très bien	very well
je vous remercie	thank you
. . . et vous(-même)?	. . . and you(rself)?
Vous êtes d'Angers?	Are you from Angers?
Vous êtes d'où?	Where are you from?
je suis d'Avignon	I'm from Avignon
Vous désirez?	What would you like?
Désirez-vous . . . ?/ Vous voulez . . . ?	Would you like . . . ?

d'accord	fine/right/OK
je vous sers tout de suite	I'll serve you right away
le thé nature	without milk or lemon
le thé au lait	tea with milk
le thé citron	tea with lemon
Que désirez-vous boire?	What would you like to drink?
une bière	beer
Bouteille ou pression (f)?	Bottle or draught?
bien sûr	of course
un porto	port
un jus d'orange	orange juice
A la vôtre/Tchin!	Your health!/Cheers!
Tu sais compter . . . ?	Can you count . . . ?
jusqu'à	up to
vas-y	go on
lentement	slowly

EXPLANATIONS

GREETINGS AND GOODBYES

Bonjour means 'hello' during the day, but say *Bonsoir* in the evening.
Au revoir means 'goodbye' at any time, or you can say *Bonsoir* in the evening.

You can add *madame, mademoiselle* or *monsieur:*
Bonjour, monsieur
Au revoir, madame

If it's someone you know, you can add their name:
Bonjour, Monsieur Bouillon
Bonsoir, Béatrice

In a café or a restaurant, you may be greeted with: *Bonjour, monsieur-dame,* or if there are several of you: *Bonsoir, messieurs-dames*. Don't be surprised if it sounds more like: *'jour, 'sieurs-dames!*

HOW ARE YOU?

To ask how someone is, say:
Comment allez-vous?
Or if it's someone you know:
Ça va?
If someone asks you how you are, you can reply:

(Oui) bien,
(Oui) je vais bien, } *merci*
(Oui) très bien,
Ça va,

People may also ask: *Vous allez bien?* Or if you don't look well: *Ça va pas?* If you're feeling under the weather, say: *Non, ça ne va pas* or just *Non, ça va pas* which is 'No I'm not feeling well'. You will often hear people leave out the *ne* in negative sentences: *Je sais pas* (I don't know); *Je peux pas* (I can't).

PLEASE AND THANK YOU

S'il vous plaît is 'please'. You use it when you ask for something, but also to attract the waiter's attention:
S'il vous plaît!
Oui? Que désirez-vous?

Merci accompanied by *beaucoup* or *bien,* is 'thank you' or 'thank you very much'. Be careful! *Merci* by itself can mean 'no thank you', if you want to decline an offer of food, for example. To make your meaning clear, say: *Oui, merci* or *Non, merci*. You can also say: *Je vous remercie*.

ORDERING DRINKS

The simplest way is to say what you want and add *s'il vous plaît*.

Un thé au lait,
Deux bières, } *s'il vous plaît*
Un citron pressé (freshly squeezed lemon juice)

MASCULINE AND FEMININE

In French, both people and things are either masculine or feminine; it's best to learn which words are which as you go along.

With masculine words, you use *un,* which is 'a' or 'an': *un thé, un citron pressé, un apéritif, un pub.* With feminine nouns, you use *une* which is also 'a' or 'an': *une bière, une bouteille, une pression, une pâtisserie.*

NUMBERS

For numbers one to ten, say:
un deux trois quatre cinq six sept huit neuf dix

Numbers are important for placing orders, dealing with prices, dates, times, hotel rooms, etc. If you don't understand them first time, ask for them to be repeated slowly: *Lentement, s'il vous plaît* or more slowly: *Plus lentement, s'il vous plaît.*

WHERE ARE YOU FROM?

To ask people where they're from, say, for example:
Vous êtes de Lille? Are you from Lille?
Vous êtes d'où? Where are you from?

To answer these questions, say:
Oui, je suis de Lille
Non, je suis d'Angers
Je suis de Chichester
If the word following *de* begins with a vowel, you shorten *de* to *d': Vous êtes d'où? Je suis d'Angers.*

NATIONALITIES

To exchange information about nationalities, you can again use *Vous êtes . . . ?* and *Je suis . . .:*
Vous êtes français? (French)
Vous êtes anglais? (English)

Vous êtes américain? (American)

If you're asking a woman, you add an *-e:*
Vous êtes écossaise? (Scottish)
Vous êtes galloise? (Welsh)
Vous êtes irlandaise? (Irish)
To answer, say:
Oui, je suis écossais(e).
Non, je suis anglais(e).

EXERCISES

1 GREETINGS

a Greet your friend Marie-Pierre and ask if she's OK.
b You meet Anne in the evening. How do you greet her?
c Say 'good morning' to Monsieur Bouillon and ask him how he is.
d Say goodbye to Monsieur Doreau.
e You've met a woman whose name you don't know. Greet her.

2 AT THE 'CAFE'

What is your side of this conversation?

VOUS	*Call the waiter.*
M. MENARD	Bonjour, monsieur-dame. Vous désirez?
VOUS	*Ask for two beers.*
M. MENARD	Bouteille ou pression?
VOUS	*Draught, please.*
M. MENARD	D'accord.

3 NUMBERS

a Fill in the missing numbers:
un deux . . . quatre . . . six . . . . . . neuf . . .

b Work out the following:
six + quatre = . . .
deux + trois = . . .
un + cinq = . . .
sept + deux = . . .
huit + deux = . . .

4 ORDERING DRINKS

Have a look at the drinks' list, then tell the waiter what you want:

BOISSONS

Thé nature	10,00 F
Thé citron	11,50 F
Café	6,00 F
Jus d'orange	11,00 F
Jus de tomatoes	11,00 F

ALCOOLS ET LIQUEURS

Cointreau	23,00 F
Cognac	23,00 F
Rhum	20,00 F

a A lemon tea, please.
b Two coffees, please.
c Three orange juices, please.
d One cointreau, please.

5 MIX AND MATCH

Match the questions and answers:

1 Vous êtes écossaise?
2 Et vous?
3 Vous êtes de Glasgow?
4 Vous êtes galloise?
5 Ça va?

a Ça va très bien merci.
b Non, je suis d'Edimbourg.
c Non, je suis française.
d Moi, je suis anglais.
e Oui, je suis de Cardiff.

WORTH KNOWING

GREETINGS AND GOODBYES

In France, greeting people is often accompanied by a handshake. If you know someone well, you're more likely to kiss each other on both cheeks – two, three or even four times, depending on local custom.

You can use *Bonjour* at any time during the day, except in the evening. It literally means 'good day' and it's used for both 'good morning' and 'good afternoon'. You may often hear *Bon après-midi*. This isn't a greeting but means 'Have a good afternoon'. Similarly, *Bonne soirée* means 'Have a good evening'.

If you're introduced to someone, you can reply *Enchanté* (Pleased to meet you) or *Bienvenu* (Welcome).

Bonsoir is used in the evening roughly after 6 p.m. You can use it both when you meet and when you leave people.

Au revoir can be used at any time to say goodbye.

People don't use first names as readily as in Britain especially when they don't know you very well. If in doubt, wait for the other person to take the first step.

Young people tend to say *Salut!*, both when they meet and when they leave each other, accompanied by kisses on the cheeks or, between men, a handshake.

DRINKS

une eau minérale mineral water
un fruit pressé freshly squeezed fruit juice (*orange, citron . . .*) (orange, lemon . . .)
un diabolo (menthe, fraise . . .) lemonade (with mint, strawberry syrup)
un jus d'ananas pineapple juice
une limonade lemonade
une pression draught beer
une bière bouteille bottled beer
un panaché lager shandy
un café crème coffee with milk
un décafeiné decaffeinated coffee
un chocolat (chaud) (hot) chocolate
une infusion (menthe, tilleul) herbal tea (mint, lime)
un pastis/un ricard spirit with aniseed
un porto blanc ou *rouge* white *or* red port

One of the ways to say 'Cheers' or 'Your health!' is *Tchin-tchin!* Other expressions include *A votre santé! A la vôtre!* or *Santé!*

2 SHOPPING

KEY WORDS AND PHRASES

je voudrais . . .	I'd like . . .
Vous avez . . . ?	Do you have . . . ?
ce sera tout	that will be all
Voulez-vous autre chose?	Would you like something else?
Qu'est-ce que vous voulez?	What would you like?
Avec ceci?	Anything else?
voilà	there you are
C'est combien?	How much is it?
Je vous dois combien?	How much do I owe you?
cela vous fait vingt-deux francs cinquante	That will be 22,50 F

CONVERSATIONS

BUYING A SIGHTSEEING GUIDE

MARIE-PIERRE Bonjour, madame.
EMPLOYEE Bonjour, madame.
MARIE-PIERRE Un guide du château, s'il vous plaît.
EMPLOYEE Bien sûr. Celui-ci?
MARIE-PIERRE Oui, très bien. Merci.

BUYING THE LOCAL LIQUEUR

BEATRICE Je voudrais une bouteille de cointreau, s'il vous plaît.

VENDEUR Une bouteille de cointreau. Une grande ou une petite?

BEATRICE Une grande.

VENDEUR Une grande bouteille. Eh bien, tenez. Voilà madame.

A BAGUETTE PLEASE

BEATRICE Bonjour, madame.

MME CHAILLOU Bonjour, madame.

BEATRICE Une baguette, s'il vous plaît.

MME CHAILLOU Oui.

BEATRICE Merci.

MME CHAILLOU Voulez-vous autre chose?

BEATRICE Non merci.

AT THE DELICATESSEN

BEATRICE Je voudrais du fromage, s'il vous plaît.

MME CHAILLOU Oui.

BEATRICE Deux cents grammes de gruyère.

MME CHAILLOU Bien . . . Avec ceci madame?

BEATRICE Je voudrais du saucisson, s'il vous plaît.

MME CHAILLOU Oui.

BEATRICE Six tranches de celui-là.

MME CHAILLOU Six tranches de celui-là. Oui. Avec ceci, madame?

BEATRICE Ce sera tout.

AT THE INDOOR MARKET

BEATRICE Un kilo de pommes, s'il vous plaît.

VENDEUSE Oui. Qu'est-ce que vous voulez? Des goldens, des . . . ?

BEATRICE	Oui, des goldens.
VENDEUSE	Des goldens? D'accord.

BUYING PETROL

POMPISTE	Bonjour, monsieur-dame.
M. BOUILLON	Bonjour, monsieur. Le plein s'il vous plaît.
POMPISTE	D'essence, de super ou de super sans plomb?
M. BOUILLON	Super sans plomb, s'il vous plaît.
POMPISTE	Merci.

GETTING FRENCH CURRENCY

MARIE-PIERRE	Je voudrais changer des travellers chèques, s'il vous plaît.
EMPLOYEE	Oui. Travellers chèques en francs français?
MARIE-PIERRE	Oui, en francs français.
EMPLOYEE	D'accord. Est-ce que vous avez votre passeport?
MARIE-PIERRE	Oui . . . Voilà!

HOW MUCH IS IT?

MARIE-PIERRE	Vous avez un plan de la ville, s'il vous plaît?
MME HOPPELER	Oui. Voilà.
MARIE-PIERRE	C'est combien?
MME HOPPELER	C'est gratuit.

AT THE POST OFFICE

M. BOUILLON	Bonjour, monsieur.
EMPLOYE	Bonjour.
M. BOUILLON	Pour envoyer une carte postale en Grande-Bretagne, c'est combien s'il vous plaît?
EMPLOYE	C'est deux francs trente.
M. BOUILLON	Très bien. Je voudrais six timbres alors.
EMPLOYE	Voilà.

M. BOUILLON — C'est combien?
EMPLOYE — Treize francs quatre-vingts.

HOW MUCH DO I OWE YOU?

BEATRICE — Je vous dois combien?
MME CHAILLOU — Cela vous fait vingt-deux francs cinquante.
BEATRICE — Oui, *(handing 30 francs)* voilà.
MME CHAILLOU — Oui, merci. Vingt-deux francs cinquante, (*giving the change*) vingt-trois, vingt-quatre, vingt-cinq et trente. Merci. Au revoir, madame.
BEATRICE — Au revoir, madame.

WORD LIST

celui-ci	this one
grand(e)	big
petit(e)	small
eh bien, tenez	here you are
le fromage	cheese
le saucisson (à l'ail)	(garlic) sausage
une tranche	slice
celui-là	that one
le plein	fill it up
l'essence (f)	two-star petrol
le super	four-star
le super sans plomb	four-star unleaded
un plan de la ville	map of the town
gratuit(e)	free (of charge)
une carte postale	postcard
la Grande-Bretagne	Great Britain
un timbre	stamp

EXPLANATIONS

SAYING WHAT YOU WANT

The shop assistant may ask:
Qu'est-ce que vous voulez?
Que voulez-vous?
Vous désirez?

Then, like ordering a drink, you can just name what you want and add 'please':

Un guide du château
Une baguette } *s'il vous plaît*
Le plein

You can also say *Je voudrais . . .* (I'd like . . .) or *Vous avez . . . ?* (Do you have . . . ?):
Je voudrais une bouteille de cointreau, s'il vous plaît
Vous avez un plan de la ville?
Vous avez des goldens?

Another way of saying 'I'd like' is *J'aimerais*
J'aimerais six tranches de saucisson, s'il vous plaît

MASCULINE AND FEMININE

You already know *un* and *une* for 'a'/'an'. 'The' is either *le* with a masculine word or *la* with a feminine word:
le guide du château
la bouteille de cointreau

PLURAL

Un and *une* become *des,* while *le* and *la* become *les:*

un *travellers chèque*	**des** *travellers chèques*
une *golden*	**des** *goldens*
la *pomme*	**les** *pommes*
le *guide du château*	**les** *guides du château*

'SOME' AND 'ANY'

'Some' and 'any' are *du, de la, de l'* or *des*. You use *du* with a masculine word, *de la* with a feminine word, *de l'* if the word begins with a vowel. With all plural words, you use *des:*

J'aimerais {
du fromage
de l'essence sans plomb
de la limonade
des timbres

Du, de la, de l' and *des* can also mean 'of the':
Un guide du château, s'il vous plaît
Vous avez un plan de la ville?

HOW MUCH DO YOU WANT?

The assistant may want to know how many (apples) you want or how many slices (of garlic sausage):
Combien en voulez-vous?
Vous voulez combien de tranches?

You might want to reply:

Un kilo de goldens	A kilo of Golden Delicious
Une livre de tomates	A pound of tomatoes
Deux cents grammes de gruyère	Two hundred grammes of gruyère
Une douzaine d'oeufs	A dozen eggs
Une bouteille d'eau minérale	A bottle of mineral water
Un paquet de biscuits	A packet of biscuits
Une brique de lait	A carton of milk

You may be offered a choice:
Grand ou petit?
Celui-ci or *Celui-là?* with masculine words
Celle-ci or *Celle-là?* with feminine words
Rouge ou blanc?
D'essence, de super ou de super sans plomb?

The assistant is almost bound to ask:

Vous voulez autre chose? *Et avec ceci?* *C'est tout?*	Anything else?

If you have all you want, you can reply:
Ce sera tout That will be all

HOW MUCH IS IT?

To find out how much you have to pay, ask:
C'est combien?
Je vous dois combien?

You can also ask:
C'est combien les goldens?
C'est combien la bouteille de cointreau?

NUMBERS

To understand prices in shops you'll need to understand numbers. (You'll find a more detailed list of numbers on page 79.)

vingt 20	*vingt et un* 21	*vingt-deux* 22	*trente* 30
quarante 40	*cinquante* 50	*soixante* 60	*cent* 100
deux cents 200	*deux cent cinquante* 250		

PRICES

They are written and spoken as follows:
20,60 F = *vingt francs soixante*
45,60 F = *quarante-cinq francs soixante*
250,30 F = *deux cent cinquante francs trente*

If you don't understand, don't panic. Just ask the assistant to write the price down:
Vous pouvez m'écrire le prix, s'il vous plaît?

EXERCISES

1 HERE'S YOUR SHOPPING LIST

Ask for each of the items on this shopping list, start with *j'aimerais* or *je voudrais* and finish with *s'il vous plaît:*

a 1 bottle of red wine
b 3 French sticks
c 450 grammes of gruyère
d 8 slices of (garlic) sausage
e 2 kilos of apples
f 1 pound of tomatoes

2 MIXED UP

You've bought the cheese, the (garlic) sausage and the apples. The shop assistant's side of the conversation is below, but it has been mixed up. Sort out the correct order, and work out the complete conversation.

a Et avec ceci?
b Qu'est-ce que vous voulez?
c Combien de kilos?
d Vous voulez autre chose?
e Combien de tranches?

3 HOW MUCH?

Put the first three prices into figures and the rest into words.

a le vin = vingt-cinq francs soixante
b la baguette = deux francs quatre-vingts

c le gruyère = quatorze francs trente-trois
d le saucisson = 15,00 F
e les pommes = 9,50 F
f les tomates = 13,29 F

4 AT THE FRUIT MARKET

What's your side of this conversation?

VENDEUSE	Bonjour monsieur.
VOUS	*Greet the stallholder. She's a young woman.*
VENDEUSE	Qu'est-ce que vous voulez?
VOUS	*You'd like a kilo of apples.*
VENDEUSE	Oui . . . Et avec ceci?
VOUS	*Six tomatoes, please.*
VENDEUSE	Voilà.
VOUS	*Thank her and ask how much the oranges are.*
VENDEUSE	Huit francs le kilo.

5 A FEW NECESSITIES!

How do you ask for them?

a Your first stop is the tourist office: you'd like a guide of Angers.
b Now to the bank: you'd like to change £200 into French francs (£1 and 1lb are both *une livre*).
c You call at the Post Office: you'd like four stamps for Britain.
d Finally, on to the petrol station: you'd like 20 litres of unleaded petrol.

WORTH KNOWING

PETROL

Petrol in France comes in three grades: *essence* or *ordinaire* (2-star), *super* (4-star) and *essence sans plomb* (unleaded petrol). You'll also come across *superplus* (improved 4-star) and *super sans plomb* (unleaded 4-star).

MONEYBOX

The *franc* (F) is divided into 100 *centimes* (c). You'll find coins of 5 c, 10 c, 20 c, ½ F, 1 F, 2 F, 5 F and 10 F. There are notes for 20 F, 50 F, 100 F, 200 F and 500 F. In shops, your bills will be rounded off to the nearest multiple of five centimes. For example, 54,27 F becomes only 54,25 F!

BREAD

There's a large variety of breads in France, all worth trying. To help you, here are a few names:

la ficelle	smaller and thinner than the baguette
la boule	a round loaf
la couronne	a loaf in the shape of a crown
le pain paillasse	leavened bread
le pain de seigle	rye bread
le pain complet	wholemeal bread
le pain aux céréales	wholemeal bread made with different sorts of grain
le pain de campagne	farmhouse bread

If you ask for *un pain* you'll be given a stick of white bread (also called *un parisien*) roughly equivalent to two baguettes.

SHOPS

You might find it useful to know the following shops:

la boucherie	butcher's
la boulangerie	baker's
la charcuterie	delicatessen
l'épicerie (f)	grocer's
la maison de la presse	newsagent's
la pharmacie	chemist's
le tabac	tobacconist's

If you don't want to go to the trouble of cooking a meal, the *charcuterie* may have all you need. There you'll find ready-prepared dishes, both hot and cold.

3 GETTING ABOUT

KEY WORDS AND PHRASES

Le centre-ville, s'il vous plaît?	The town centre, please?
Il y un parking près d'ici?	Is there a car-park nearby?
Pour aller à la cathédrale?	How do I get to the cathedral?
à droite	on/to the right
à gauche	on/to the left
là-bas	over there
vous prenez . . .	you take . . .
la première rue à droite	the first road on the right
la deuxième à gauche	the second on the left
tout droit	straight ahead
Quelle heure est-il?	what's time time?
A quelle heure ferme le château?	what time does the castle close?
C'est ouvert quand?	when is it open?
un aller simple	a single ticket
un aller-retour	a return ticket

CONVERSATIONS

THE TOWN CENTRE, PLEASE?

MARIE-PIERRE Pardon, monsieur.
PASSANT Oui.
MARIE-PIERRE Le centre-ville, s'il vous plaît?
PASSANT Alors, c'est très facile. Vous prenez la

	deuxième à gauche . . .
MARIE-PIERRE	Oui.
PASSANT	Et ensuite c'est tout droit.

AND IS IT FAR FROM HERE?

MARIE-PIERRE	Et c'est loin d'ici?
PASSANT	Non. Environ deux minutes à pied.
MARIE-PIERRE	D'accord, merci beaucoup. Au revoir, monsieur.
PASSANT	Je vous en prie. Au revoir.

IS THERE A BANK NEARBY?

MARIE-PIERRE	Excusez-moi, monsieur. Il y a une banque près d'ici?
PASSANT	Une banque . . . Oui, le Crédit Lyonnais est là-bas, la deuxième rue à droite.
MARIE-PIERRE	Et c'est loin d'ici?
PASSANT	Oh, non. C'est à deux cents mètres.
MARIE-PIERRE	D'accord. Merci beaucoup.
PASSANT	De rien.
MARIE-PIERRE	Au revoir, monsieur.
PASSANT	Au revoir.

SORRY, I'M NOT FROM HERE!

PIERRICK	Pardon, madame. Il y a un parking près d'ici?
PASSANTE	Ah, désolée. Je ne suis pas d'ici.
PIERRICK	Ah, ça ne fait rien. Merci.

LOOKING FOR A PETROL STATION

PIERRICK	Pardon, madame. Il y a une station d'essence près d'ici?
PASSANTE	Oui. Vous prenez sur votre droite . . .
PIERRICK	Oui.
PASSANTE	Et la station est tout de suite à gauche.
PIERRICK	Et c'est loin, non?
PASSANTE	Non, à peu près cinq cents mètres.

HOW DO I GET TO THE CATHEDRAL, PLEASE?

MARIE-PIERRE Pardon, madame. Pour aller à la cathédrale, s'il vous plaît?

MME CHAILLOU Pour aller à la cathédrale . . . Alors, de la rue Bressigny, vous traversez le boulevard Foch.

MARIE-PIERRE Oui.

MME CHAILLOU Vous suivez la rue Saint Aubin, la rue piétonne.

MARIE-PIERRE Oui.

MME CHAILLOU Et vous arrivez à la cathédrale.

AT THE TOURIST INFORMATION OFFICE

MARIE-PIERRE Le musée David d'Angers, c'est où?

MME HOPPELER Eh bien, il est tout près d'ici, sur votre droite.

MARIE-PIERRE Et c'est ouvert quand, s'il vous plaît?

MME HOPPELER C'est ouvert tous les jours . . .

MARIE-PIERRE Mmmn . . .

MME HOPPELER De neuf heures à douze heures et de quatorze heures à dix-huit heures.

TWO TICKETS FOR THE CASTLE, PLEASE

PIERRICK Deux tickets pour le château, s'il vous plaît.

EMPLOYEE Oui. Voilà. Quarante-six francs, s'il vous plaît.

PIERRICK Voilà.

EMPLOYEE Merci. Alors quarante-six, quarante-huit, cinquante; une, deux, trois, quatre et cinq qui vous font cent.

PIERRICK Merci beaucoup. Et à quelle heure ferme le château?

EMPLOYEE Dix-sept heures trente.

WHAT'S THE TIME, PLEASE?

MARIE-PIERRE Pardon, monsieur. Quelle heure est-il, s'il vous plaît?

PASSANT Il est trois heures moins dix.

MARIE-PIERRE Merci.

PASSANT Je vous en prie.

BUYING TRAIN TICKETS

PIERRICK Je voudrais deux aller-retour pour Nantes s'il vous plaît.

EMPLOYE Oui monsieur. En première ou en seconde classe?

PIERRICK En seconde, s'il vous plaît.

EMPLOYE Bien monsieur. Voilà. Deux cent huit francs, s'il vous plaît.

PIERRICK Voilà.

EMPLOYE Je vous remercie.

A SINGLE TO PARIS, PLEASE

MARIE-PIERRE Je voudrais un aller simple pour Paris, s'il vous plaît.

EMPLOYE Oui. En première ou en seconde classe?

MARIE-PIERRE En seconde classe.

EMPLOYE Bien. Cent cinquante-quatre francs, s'il vous plaît.

WORD LIST

facile easy
ensuite then
environ about
à pied on foot
je vous en prie my pleasure/you're welcome
là-bas (over) there

à deux cents mètres	200 metres away
la station d'essence	petrol station
vous prenez sur votre droite	you turn right
tout de suite à gauche	just on the left
à peu près cinq cents mètres	about 500 metres
alors	well
de la rue Bressigny	from the rue Bressigny
vous traversez	you cross
vous suivez	you follow
la rue piétonne	the pedestrian street
tout près d'ici	very near here
sur votre droite	on your right
qui vous font cent	which make 100
en première ou en seconde classe?	first or second class?

EXPLANATIONS

ASKING THE WAY

The simplest way is to name the place you want to get to and add 'please':

le centre-ville
la cathédrale   *s'il vous plaît?*
le musée

You can also start with *pour aller à . . .:*

à la cathédrale
au château
Pour aller à l'hôtel   *s'il vous plaît?*
aux toilettes
à Nantes

Notice that you use *à la* if the word is feminine, *au* (= *à* + *le*) if it's masculine, *à l'* if it begins with a vowel or an 'h' which is not pronounced, and *aux* (= *à* + *les*) if it's plural.

To stop a passer-by in the street, say:

Pardon, monsieur / *Excusez-moi, madame* } *le centre-ville, s'il vous plaît?*

If you want to know where a place is, the key word is *où:*
Le musée, c'est où?
C'est où la gare, s'il vous plaît?
Où est le musée, s'il vous plaît?

To ask how far or near the place is, say:
C'est loin d'ici?
Il y a une pharmacie près d'ici?

The answer is likely to include a time or a distance:
Non, environ deux minutes à pied No, about two minutes' walk
Oh, non. C'est à deux cents mètres Oh no. It's 200 metres away
C'est à une heure en voiture It's an hour's drive away

DIRECTIONS

No matter how you travel, the basic directions are the same:

tout droit straight ahead
la première à droite first right
la deuxième sur votre gauche the second on your left

Here are some more useful expressions. On the map below, follow the directions given overleaf.

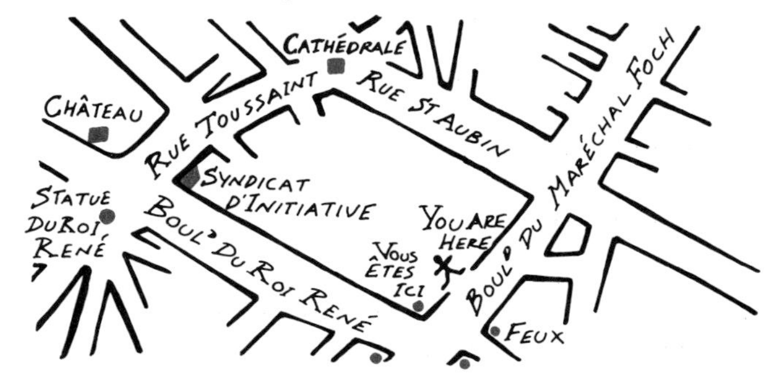

You're on the Boulevard du Maréchal Foch.
– *Pour aller à la cathédrale, s'il vous plaît?*
– *Vous prenez* (take) *la première rue sur votre gauche et vous continuez tout droit. La cathédrale est devant* (in front) *vous.*
– *Pour aller au château, s'il vous plaît?*
– *Vous tournez à droite aux feux* (traffic lights). *Puis vous allez tout droit jusqu'à* (as far as) *la statue du Roi René* (the statue of King René). *Et voilà, le château!*
– *Pour aller au syndicat d'initiative, s'il vous plaît?*
– *Le syndicat d'initiative? C'est juste à côté* (next to) *du château*

FIRST, SECOND, THIRD . . .

'First' is *premier* with a masculine word or *première* with a feminine word. Otherwise you normally add *-ième* to the cardinal number: *deux**ième**, trois**ième**.*

There are three exceptions, however. With *vingt et un, trente et un,* etc., 'first' becomes *-unième,* producing *vingt et unième, trente et unième,* etc. An 'e' at the end of the cardinal number is dropped: *quatre* becomes *quatrième, onze* becomes *onzième.* Finally the 'f' at the end of *neuf* becomes *v,* producing *neuvième.*

WHAT'S THE TIME

To find out what the time is, ask: *Quelle heure est-il?*

To tell someone the time, start with *Il est:*

Il est huit heures	It's eight o'clock
huit heures cinq	five past . . .
huit heures et quart	quarter past . . .
huit heures et demie	half past . . .
huit heures moins le quart	quarter to . . .
huit heures moins dix	ten to . . .

The 24-hour clock is also frequently used, and not only in official situations:

Le train part à quinze heures seize (15.16)
Il arrive à dix-huit heures trente-neuf (18.39)

In the 24-hour clock, midday is *douze heures* and midnight is *zéro heure:*
Le train part à douze heures quinze
Il arrive à zéro heure neuf

Otherwise, it's either *midi* (midday) or *minuit* (midnight); a.m. is *du matin (il est dix heures du matin);* p.m. is *de l'après-midi* till 6 p.m. or *du soir* thereafter *(il est cinq heures de l'après-midi/il est neuf heures du soir).*

WHAT TIME DOES IT OPEN/CLOSE?

To ask when a place opens or closes:
A quelle heure ouvre la pharmacie?
A quelle heure ferme la banque?

You can also say:
Le musée, c'est ouvert quand?

To find out whether a place is open or shut, just say:
C'est ouvert? C'est fermé?

GOING BY TRAIN

To buy a train ticket, say for example:
Un aller-simple pour Le Mans en seconde, s'il vous plaît
A second-class single to Le Mans, please
un aller-simple a single
un aller-retour a return
pour (Nantes, Paris) to (Nantes, Paris)
en première first class
en seconde second class

To enquire whether there's a train for Nantes at 8.00:
Il y a un train pour Nantes à huit heures?
To enquire about train departures:
A quelle heure part le train pour Nantes?
To find out at what time the train arrives:
Il arrive à quelle heure?
To find out which platform the train leaves from:
C'est quel quai pour . . . ?

DAYS OF THE WEEK

Starting with Sunday, they are:
dimanche, lundi, mardi, mercredi, jeudi, vendredi, samedi

Note that in French, initial capital letters are not needed.

EXERCISES

1 DIRECTIONS

Work out the questions and answers using the map and prompts below.

EXAMPLE

You want to go from the Jardin du Mail to the Pub St Aubin.

– *Pour aller du Jardin du Mail au Pub St Aubin, s'il vous plaît?*

– *Vous prenez le Boulevard du Maréchal Foch sur la gauche et vous tournez dans la quatrième rue à droite.*

You want to go . . .

a From the cathedral to the castle.

b From the Tourist Information Office to the Jardin du Mail.

c From the Pub St Aubin to the Musée David d'Angers.

2 WHAT TIME IS IT?

How would you say each of these times in French?

a 10.25 a.m. **b** 1.40 p.m. **c** 4.05 a.m. **d** 9.30 p.m.
e 15.10 **f** 13.15 **g** 21.35 **h** 00.42

3 HOW DO I GET TO . . . ?

You stop a passer-by to ask the way to the castle. What do you say?

VOUS *Excuse-me.*

PASSANT Oui?

VOUS *How do I get to the castle, please?*

PASSANT C'est très facile. Vous prenez le boulevard du Maréchal Foch jusqu'au boulevard du Roi René, sur votre droite . . .

VOUS *Sorry. More slowly, please.*

PASSANT Alors tout droit. Puis le boulevard du Roi René à droite.

VOUS *On the left . . . the boulevard of the Roi René . . .*

PASSANT Non. A droite. Et c'est tout droit.

VOUS *OK. And is it far?*

PASSANT Non. Dix minutes à pied.

VOUS *Fine. Thank you very much.*

PASSANT Je vous en prie.

VOUS *Goodbye.*

4 BOOKING TRAIN TICKETS

What would you say to book the following tickets?

EXAMPLE *Un aller simple pour Tours, en seconde.*

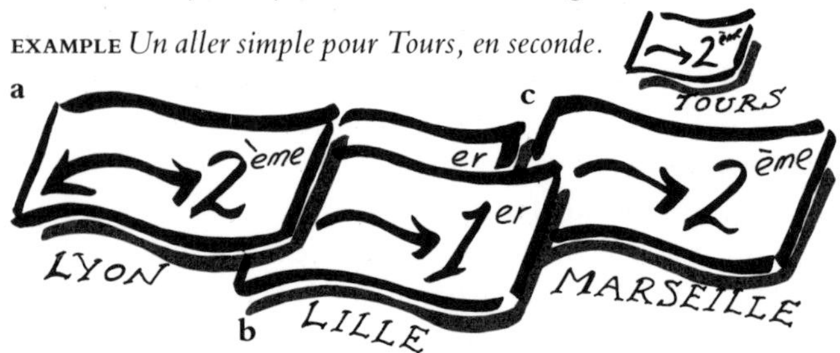

You're now making enquiries about going to Saumur.

d Ask whether there's a train for Saumur at 10.00.
e Ask which platform the train leaves from.
f Ask how much a first-class return ticket is.

5 OPENING AND CLOSING TIMES

When can you visit each of these places?

a *Musée:* ouvert de 10 h jusqu'à 17 h 30; fermé le dimanche.
b *Château:* ouvert de 9 h 30 jusqu'à 18 h; fermé le lundi.
c *Cathédrale:* ouvert tous les jours de 9 h jusqu'à 18 h.

WORTH KNOWING

TRAVELLING BY ROAD, BY TRAIN AND ON FOOT

Roads in France are divided into three main categories:
'A': *autoroute* (motorway)
'N': *nationale* ('A' road)
'D': *départementale* ('B' road)

In summer, main French roads can be very busy. Each year, the French authorities run a special information service called

Bison Futé (the cunning buffalo) to help holidaymakers avoid congested areas (*les points noirs*) and traffic jams (*les bouchons*). They recommend alternative routes called *Itinéraires Bis* and relief routes called *Itinéraires de délestage*. You can get maps at service stations or toll points on the motorway. Otherwise, information is given on the radio.

Here are some useful driving expressions:

priorité à droite give way to the right
stationnement interdit no parking
chaussée déformée uneven road surface
horodateur parking meter
travaux roadworks
déviation diversion

As an alternative to motoring, you may want to take the train. France's railway network is the SNCF (*Société Nationale des Chemins de Fer français)*; trains are generally modern and comfortable, with a well-stocked buffet car – and are invariably on time, too. You could try the TGV (*train à grande vitesse*), France's high-speed train. You'll need to book your seat in advance and pay a small booking fee (*un supplément*).

In the railway station itself, look out for the following signs: *GUICHET* (ticket office), *RENSEIGNEMENTS* (information office), *DEPARTS ET ARRIVEES* (departures and arrivals), *SALLE D'ATTENTE* (waiting room), *CONSIGNE* (left-luggage), and *ACCES AUX QUAIS* (access to platforms).

Before getting on any train, your ticket must be validated (*composter*): *le compostage du ticket* is compulsory if you don't want to be fined.

If you want to explore France at a more leisurely pace, you may choose to travel on *les sentiers* or *les chemins de grande randonnée* (long-distance footpaths) and stay at a *gîte d'étapes* (night stop-over houses). On maps, the long-distance footpaths are indicated *'GR'* followed by a number (*GR2*) for example.

4 FINDING SOMEWHERE TO STAY

KEY WORDS AND PHRASES

Vous avez . . .	Do you have . . .
des chambres de libre?	rooms available
de la place de libre	space available (in campsite)
Je voudrais réserver . . .	I'd like to book . . .
une chambre à un grand lit	a room with a double bed
avec douche/bain/cabinet de toilette	with shower/bath/washing facilities
J'ai . . .	I have . . .
une réservation	a reservation
une caravane/une tente	a caravan/a tent
pour ce soir	for tonight
pour la semaine prochaine	for next week
pour trois nuits	for three nights
du trois au six mai	from 3 to 6 May
je voudrais la clef numéro neuf	I'd like key number 9
A quelle heure est-ce que vous servez le petit déjeuner?	What time do you serve breakfast?

CONVERSATIONS

DO YOU HAVE ROOMS AVAILABLE?

PIERRICK Bonsoir, monsieur.

M. OCHER Bonsoir, monsieur.

PIERRICK — Vous avez des chambres de libre s'il vous plaît?
M. OCHER — Pour ce soir?
PIERRICK — Oui, pour ce soir.
M. OCHER — Oui, monsieur. Bien sûr. Que désirez-vous? Une chambre avec bain, douche ou cabinet de toilette?
PIERRICK — Avec douche, s'il vous plaît.

WHAT TIME DO YOU SERVE BREAKFAST?

PIERRICK — A quelle heure est-ce que vous servez le petit déjeuner, s'il vous plaît?
M. OCHER — A partir de sept heures.
PIERRICK — Jusqu'à quelle heure?
M. OCHER — Jusqu'à dix heures.
PIERRICK — D'accord. Merci.

MAKING AN ADVANCE BOOKING

PIERRICK — Je voudrais réserver une chambre à un grand lit, s'il vous plaît, pour la semaine prochaine.
M. OCHER — Oui, monsieur. Que désirez-vous? Avec bain, douche ou cabinet de toilette?
PIERRICK — Avec bain, s'il vous plaît.
M. OCHER — Avec bain. Pour quelles dates?
PIERRICK — Du trois au six mai, s'il vous plaît.

CHECKING THE PRICE

PIERRICK — Et c'est combien?
M. OCHER — Deux cent dix francs pour une personne, deux cent vingt francs pour deux personnes.
PIERRICK — Et le petit déjeuner est compris?
M. OCHER — Non, en supplément, vingt-quatre francs.
PIERRICK — D'accord. Ça va.

SPELLING YOUR NAME

M. OCHER — Quel est votre nom?

PIERRICK	Alors, je m'appelle Monsieur Picot. P-I-C-O-T.
M. OCHER	Monsieur Picot. Très bien, monsieur. C'est inscrit.
PIERRICK	Je vous remercie.

ARRIVING AT THE HOTEL

MARIE-PIERRE	Bonjour, monsieur.
M. OCHER	Bonjour, madame.
MARIE-PIERRE	J'ai une réservation, je crois.
M. OCHER	Oui, pour ce soir?
MARIE-PIERRE	Oui, pour ce soir.
M. OCHER	On va regarder. Quel est votre nom?
MARIE-PIERRE	Méchineau.
M. OCHER	Ah, oui. Madame Méchineau. Vous avez la chambre numéro neuf, madame. Au deuxième étage.
MARIE-PIERRE	D'accord.

IS THERE A MESSAGE FOR ME?

PIERRICK	Est-ce qu'il y a un message pour moi?
M. OCHER	Non, il n'y a pas de message, monsieur.
PIERRICK	Rien du tout?
M. OCHER	Rien du tout.
PIERRICK	Ça ne fait rien.

ASKING FOR THE KEY

MARIE-PIERRE	Bonsoir, monsieur.
M. OCHER	Bonsoir, madame.
MARIE-PIERRE	Je voudrais la clef pour la chambre numéro neuf, s'il vous plaît.
M. OCHER	Voici, madame.
MARIE-PIERRE	Merci.

STAYING AN EXTRA NIGHT

MARIE-PIERRE	Vous avez une chambre pour ce soir?

M. OCHER Oh non, malheureusement. Nous sommes complets, madame.

MARIE-PIERRE Ah! Bon. Tant pis!

PAYING THE BILL

MARIE-PIERRE Je peux vous payer?

M. OCHER Oui, bien sûr. Je vais préparer votre note, madame.

MARIE-PIERRE D'accord.

M. OCHER Alors c'est la chambre numéro neuf?

MARIE-PIERRE Oui.

M. OCHER Vous avez trois nuits à cent quatre-vingt-quinze francs, cinq cent quatre-vingt-cinq francs.

MARIE-PIERRE Oui.

M. OCHER Trois petits déjeuners, soixante-douze francs. Pas de téléphone?

MARIE-PIERRE Pas de téléphone, non, non.

M. OCHER Alors ça vous fait sept . . . quinze . . . six cent cinquante-cinq francs. (He's rounding it down.)

BOOKING IN AT THE CAMPSITE

PIERRICK Vous avez de la place, s'il vous plaît?

RECEPTIONNISTE Bien sûr, oui. C'est pour une nuit, monsieur?

PIERRICK Non, pour trois nuits.

RECEPTIONNISTE Ah, pour trois nuits. Oui. Alors, vous avez une caravane ou une tente?

PIERRICK Une caravane.

RECEPTIONNISTE Oui. Vous êtes combien de personnes?

PIERRICK Quatre personnes. Deux adultes et deux enfants. Et c'est combien la nuit?

RECEPTIONNISTE Alors, ça vous fera quarante-sept francs cinquante pour quatre personnes, plus l'électricité vingt-trois francs cinquante.

WORD LIST

à partir de	from
jusqu'à	until/up to
Pour quelles dates?	For which dates?
c'est possible	it's possible
je m'appelle . . .	my name is . . .
c'est inscrit	it's booked
on va regarder	we'll have a look
Quel est votre nom?	What's your name?
numéro neuf	number nine
au deuxième étage	on the second floor
malheureusement	unfortunately
tant pis	never mind
Je peux vous payer?	Can I pay you?
je vais préparer votre note	I'll just prepare your bill
ça vous fait . . .	That's . . .
un enfant	a child
ça vous fera . . .	That will be

EXPLANATIONS

BOOKING A HOTEL OR CAMPSITE

To ask if any rooms/spaces are available:

Vous avez {
des chambres de libre?
une chambre pour ce soir?
de la place, s'il vous plaît?

To specify which kind of room:

Je voudrais une chambre {
avec bain/douche/cabinet de toilette
à or *avec un grand lit*
à deux lits
avec un petit lit d'enfant

At the campsite, say:

Nous avons { *une tente* / *une caravane* / *une canadienne* (a small ridge tent)

Checking in at the hotel:
J'ai une réservation

FOR HOW LONG?

When making your booking, you will be asked how long you want to stay:
Pour quelles dates? For which dates?
Pour combien de nuits? For how many nights?
Pour combien de temps? For how long?

To give the length of your stay, say:
Pour une nuit For one night
Pour quatre nuits For four nights
Pour une semaine For a week

From . . . to . . .
You can say *de . . . à* or *à partir de . . . jusqu'à . . .*:
A partir de sept heures jusqu'à dix heures
To give the exact dates, use *du . . . au* or *à partir du . . . jusqu'au . . . .*
Du trois au six mai or *à partir du trois mai jusqu'au six mai.*

HOW MUCH IS IT?

To ask how much the room is, say:
C'est combien la chambre?
C'est combien la chambre avec douche/bain s'il vous plaît?

If you want to ask whether breakfast is included:
Le petit déjeuner est compris?

Most of the time, it won't be included and the receptionist will answer:
Non, c'est en supplément or *en plus* or *en sus,* which means 'No, it's extra'.

NO, THERE'S NO MESSAGE

To say 'there isn't . . .' or that something 'is not so', you use *ne* and *pas*. They usually come either side of the verb:
Non, je ne suis pas d'Angers
Ce n'est pas possible

With *il y a,* however, *ne* comes before the *y:*
Non, il n'y a pas de message, monsieur

In spoken French, the *ne* often gets lost, so you'll hear, for example:
Je 'suis pas d'Angers
C'est pas possible
'Y a pas de message
'Pas de téléphone

SPELLING YOUR NAME

It can be very useful to know how to spell your name. To practise, listen to the cassette and have a look at the pronunciation guide (page 76). If, like Pierrick, you have a double letter in your name, use *deux* to say double:

P-I-E-deux R-I-C-K

EXERCISES

1 BOOKING HOTEL ROOMS

Ask for each of the following:

a two rooms with a double bed and a bath for three nights
b one room with twin beds and a shower for tonight
c one single room with washing facilities from 9 to 12 August
d one room with double bed and a child's bed, with shower for next week
e one room with a shower for one child and one room with a bath for two adults

2 MIX AND MATCH

Match the questions with the correct answers.

1 Est-ce que vous avez des chambres de libre?
2 Le petit déjeuner est compris?
3 Il y a un message pour moi, s'il vous plaît?
4 C'est pour combien de nuits?

a Rien du tout monsieur.
b Pour six nuits.
c Oui, monsieur.
d Non, c'est en plus.

3 SPEAKING TO THE RECEPTIONIST

Ask the hotel receptionist:

a if they've got any rooms available
b the price of a room with washing facilities
c if breakfast is included
d at what time breakfast is served

4 THERE MUST BE SOME MISTAKE!

You've made a reservation, but there's been a mistake and the hotel is full. What do you say?

VOUS *Good evening*
RECEPTIONNISTE Bonsoir, monsieur-dame.
VOUS *Say you've got a reservation for a room with a double bed and a shower.*
RECEPTIONNISTE Oui, c'est quel nom, s'il vous plaît?
VOUS *Tell him your name's Stuart.*
RECEPTIONNISTE Mmm. . . Stuart. Non. Je suis désolé. Il n'y a pas de chambre dans votre nom.
VOUS *Say you don't understand.*
RECEPTIONNISTE Non, monsieur-dame. Je suis désolé,
VOUS *Ask if there's another hotel nearby.*
RECEPTIONNISTE Oui, il y a l'Hôtel de France. Je vais téléphoner pour vous.
VOUS *Thank him.*

5 FILL THE GAPS

Can you fill in this campsite form using the information below?

Your name is Liz Paine; you are staying for seven nights as from 23 July; your vehicle number is – 789 ABC; you have one caravan and one tent; there are two adults and three children; electricity is required; your passport number is 934507 D.

CAMPING MUNICIPAL DU LAC DE MAINE
FICHE DE RENSEIGNEMENTS

Nom: ....

Prénom: ....

Numéro du passeport: ....

Numéro d'immatriculation du véhicule: ....

Nombre de personnes: .... adultes ....

enfants ....

Caravane: ....

Tente: ....

Electricité: (oui/non) ....

Nombres de nuits: ....

Dates: ....

WORTH KNOWING

In France, hotels are graded from one to five stars. Some have the letters 'NN' (*nouvelles normes*) after the stars, as well as the relevant year. The Hôtel du Mail, for example, displays '★★ NN 1990'. Yearly classification ensures that hotels comply with the grading specifications.

An alternative to hotels is the continental B&B, known as *une chambre d'hôte*. Sometimes, owners also offer a *table d'hôte,* which means that you can have your evening meal there too. In popular areas, you may need to book in advance. Ask the local tourist office (*le syndicat d'initiative*), which will give you all the relevant information.

Renting a *gîte* can also be an ideal way of spending a holiday in France. *Gîtes* are self-catering accommodation, ranging from cottages to flats, and are graded with one to three ears of corn.

Campsites are also rated from one to four stars according to the facilities they offer. Most towns and villages will have their *camping municipal*. You can also try *le camping à la ferme;* these campsites are run by local farmers who let one of their fields close to the farm. They tend to be very small and offer only basic facilities, but an attraction is the fresh farm produce (*produits de la ferme*) such as eggs (*oeufs*), milk (*lait*) and vegetables *(légumes*), which are often readily available.

5 EATING OUT

KEY WORDS AND PHRASES

Est-ce que vous avez une table pour trois, s'il vous plaît?	Do you have a table for three, please?
Vous prenez un menu ou la carte?	Will you have a set meal or choose from the à la carte list?
Vous avez choisi?	Have you chosen?
en/comme entrée	as a starter
trois menus à cent vingt, s'il vous plaît	three set meals at 120,00 F (each), please
la carte, s'il vous plaît	the menu, please
avec les escargots	with the snails
un Anjou blanc	a white Anjou
l'addition, s'il vous plaît	the bill, please

CONVERSATIONS

ASKING FOR THE MENU

PIERRICK Excusez-moi!
M. MENARD Oui?
PIERRICK La carte, s'il vous plaît.
M. MENARD Voilà, monsieur.

SET MEAL OR A LA CARTE?

PIERRICK	Marie-Pierre, vous prenez un menu ou à la carte?
MARIE-PIERRE	Je vais prendre un menu à soixante.

A LA CARTE . . .

PIERRICK	Qu'est-ce que vous prenez, Marie-Pierre?
MARIE-PIERRE	Un bon steak saignant pour moi.
PIERRICK	Et comme légumes? Des pommes frites, des haricots verts, des flageolets . . . ?
MARIE PIERRE	Des pommes frites. Des pommes frites et une salade verte.
PIERRICK	Et pour moi, un bon steak à point et des haricots verts.

AT THE PATISSERIE

MME GABORIAU	Comme pâtisseries, monsieur-dame?
MARIE-PIERRE	Hmmn . . .
MME GABORIAU	Une viennoiserie, une spécialité?
MARIE-PIERRE	Non, un pain au chocolat pour moi.
MME GABORIAU	Oui, Chaud? froid?
MARIE-PIERRE	Chaud.
MME GABORIAU	Chaud, d'accord. Et pour monsieur?
PIERRICK	Un pain aux raisins, s'il vous plaît.
MME GABORIAU	Chaud également?
PIERRICK	Oui, s'il vous plaît.

ASKING FOR A TABLE

MARC	Bonsoir, monsieur.
M. VEGER	Bonsoir, messieurs-dame.
MARIE-PIERRE	Bonsoir, monsieur.
PIERRICK	Bonsoir, monsieur.
MARC	Est-ce que vous avez une table pour trois personnes, s'il vous plaît?
M. VEGER	Oui, bien sûr.

AN APERITIF?

M. VEGER	Désirez-vous prendre des apéritifs, messieurs-dame?
MARC	Oui, certainement.
PIERRICK	Oui, bien sûr.
MARIE-PIERRE	Oui.
M. VEGER	Nous faisons des kirs au muscadet à la crème de pêche, crème de mûre, crème de cassis, ricard, cinquante et un, martini . . .
MARC	Marie-Pierre?
MARIE-PIERRE	Eh bien, un kir royal, s'il vous plaît.
M. VEGER	Oui.
PIERRICK	Et pour moi, un petit whisky.
MARC	Et un ricard.

ORDERING A SET MEAL

M. VEGER	Avez-vous choisi, messieurs-dame?
TOUS	Oui.
MARC	Alors, trois menus à cent vingt, s'il vous plaît . . .
M. VEGER	Bien, monsieur. En entrée, vous prendrez?
MARC	. . . avec en entrée, trois escargots . . .
M. VEGER	Trois escargots, oui.
MARC	Puis deux filets mignons, et Marie-Pierre?
MARIE-PIERRE	Une sole meunière pour moi.

SOME WINE?

M. VEGER	Avez-vous choisi les vins, messieurs-dame?
MARC	Oui. Alors avec les escargots, un Anjou blanc.
M. VEGER	Oui.
MARC	Et ensuite un Chinon, s'il vous plaît.
M. VEGER	Bien, monsieur.

ORDERING DESSERT

M. VEGER — Qu'est-ce que vous avez choisi comme desserts, messieurs-dame?

MARIE-PIERRE — Eh bien, une Forêt-Noire au chocolat pour moi.

M. VEGER — Oui, madame.

PIERRICK — Pour moi, une . . . pêche melba.

M. VEGER — Oui, monsieur.

MARC — Et moi, une Forêt-Noire aussi.

COFFEES OR LIQUEURS?

M. VEGER — Messieurs-dame, désirez-vous prendre des cafés ou des digestifs?

MARC — Ah, des cafés, oui. Un, deux, trois?

MARIE-PIERRE — Un café pour moi, oui.

PIERRICK — Non, pas pour moi, merci.

MARC — Alors deux cafés, s'il vous plaît. Et est-ce que vous voulez un digestif?

PIERRICK — Un petit cognac pour moi.

MARC — Et un cointreau pour moi.

M. VEGER — Bien, monsieur.

THE BILL, PLEASE

MARC — S'il vous plaît!

M. VEGER — Oui, monsieur?

MARC — L'addition, s'il vous plaît.

M. VEGER — Bien sûr, monsieur.

WORD LIST

je vais prendre	I'm going to have
saignant(e)	rare (steak)
les pommes frites (f)	French fries
les haricots verts (m)	French beans
les flageolets (m)	dwarf kidney beans
une salade verte	green salad
à point	medium (steak)
les pâtisseries (f)	cakes and pastries
la viennoiserie	Viennese pastry
la spécialité	speciality
le pain au chocolat	pastry with chocolate in the middle
le pain au raisins	pastry with currants
également	also
certainement	certainly
nous faisons des kirs	normally we do kirs (a kir is white wine with blackcurrant liqueur although you may be offered alternative liqueurs)
la crème de pêche	peach liqueur
la crème de mûre	blackberry liqueur
la crème de cassis	blackcurrant liqueur
le cinquante et un	aniseed-based aperitif
le ricard	aniseed-based aperitif
Eh bien	Well
un kir royal	champagne or sparkling wine with (normally) blackcurrant liqueur
En entrée, vous prendrez?	What will you have as a starter?
le filet mignon	pork fillet
la sole meunière	sole fried in butter, served with lemon and parsley
ensuite	then

EXPLANATIONS

THE WAITER'S QUESTIONS

To take your order, the waiter may ask:
Vous avez choisi?
Qu'est-ce que vous désirez?
Qu'est-ce que vous prenez?
Replies:
Le menu à cent vingt
Un kir royal
Le menu à soixante

Then the waiter will ask you about the starter, the main dish and the wine:
Comme entrée? or, less commonly, *en entrée?*
Et comme plat principal?
Et comme vin?
Some replies:
Trois escargots
Deux filets mignons
Un Anjou blanc

To find out about your main course, the waiter may ask:
Et comme poisson? (fish)
Et comme viande? (meat)
Replies:
Une sole meunière
Un bon steak saignant

GETTING A TABLE

To ask for a table and to say how many of you there are:
Une table pour trois personnes s'il vous plaît
Une table pour trois

Restaurants have one or two set meals (*menus*) displayed with the prices and the à la carte list.
If you've chosen a set meal, give the number of people wanting it and its price:
Deux menus à cent vingt-cinq (125,000 F)

If you've decided to eat à la carte, you'll have to answer the waiter's questions (see above) or say:
Alors, comme entrée, je vais prendre/je voudrais les escargots et comme plat principal la sole meunière
If you're not quite sure what a particular dish is, ask:
Qu'est-ce que c'est?

ABOUT QUESTIONS

A statement can also be a question, depending on the intonation used. Raising the intonation at the end of a sentence turns it into a question:
Vous avez une table pour trois?
Vous prenez un/l'apéritif?

You can also begin with *Est-ce que . . . :*
Est-ce que vous avez une table pour trois?
Est-ce que vous voulez un digestif?
Some questions begin with the verb:
Avez-vous une table pour trois?
Avez-vous choisi les vins?
Others begin with a question word:
Que désirez-vous?
Qu'est-ce que c'est?
Où est le restaurant La Treille?

THE BILL, PLEASE

To ask for the bill, say:
L'addition, s'il vous plaît!
If you want to know whether service is included, ask:
Le service est compris?

FLAVOURS AND INGREDIENTS

These are usually positioned after *au* (= *à* + *le*), *à la* or *aux* (= *à* + *les*):
un pain au chocolat
un pain aux raisins
un kir à la crème de pêche
un kir à la crème de cassis
un sandwich au jambon (ham sandwich)

ADJECTIVES

Adjectives usually come after the noun they describe:
un Anjou blanc
un steak saignant
un kir royal

A few very common ones come before the noun:
un bon steak
un petit cognac
un grand lit

Most adjectives describing feminine nouns add an *e:*
une Forêt-Noire
une salade verte
une grande bouteille

In the plural, adjectives normally take an *-s* at the end (but remember, there are many exceptions):
deux steaks saignants
trois salades vertes

EXERCISES

1 WHICH WOULD YOU CHOOSE?

1 You fancy a snack:
a un kir royal **b** un escargot **c** un sandwich au jambon

2 You've given up alcohol:
a un citron pressé **b** un cinquante et un **c** un ricard

3 You don't eat meat:
a un steak saignant **b** un filet mignon
c une sole meunière

4 You had a huge meal but can't resist a light sweet:
a une Forêt-Noire **b** une pêche melba
c une glace à la vanille

5 You want something to warm you up:
a un pain au chocolat chaud **b** un gâteau à la crème
c un pain aux raisins

2 WHAT DID THEY ORDER?

What did Marc, Marie-Pierre and Pierrick order at La Treille? Read the conversations again and make a list in French of the aperitifs, starters, etc ordered by each person starting with the aperitif, the starter, etc.

3 IN A RESTAURANT

Ask for:

a A table for three, please.
b One set meal at 75,00 F and two at 140,00 F.
c A martini, a whisky, and a white wine and blackcurrant liqueur for me.
d Two steaks (one rare, one medium) and one sole fried in butter.
e One bottle of white Anjou.
f Three peach melbas.
g Two black coffees and a white one.
h The bill, please.

4 FILL THE GAPS

a un sandwich . . . saucisson
b un gâteau . . . crème
c un thé . . . citron
d une glace . . . vanille
e un café . . . lait
f une menthe . . . eau
g un kir . . . crème de mûre

5 MIXED UP!

Put this jumbled dialogue between the waiter and yourself in the right order.

a Qu'est-ce que vous avez choisi comme vin, madame?
b Le menu à quatre-vingts, s'il vous plaît.
c Un rosé d'Anjou, s'il vous plaît.
d Et désirez-vous prendre un café?
e Un steak au poivre . . . saignant.
f Vous avez choisi un dessert, madame?
g Et ensuite?
h Non, merci. Ça va.
i Bien, madame. Que prenez-vous comme entrée?
j Oui, une pêche melba.
k Un melon au porto, s'il vous plaît.
l Avez-vous choisi, madame?

6 MIX AND MATCH

1 verte
2 blanc
3 saignant
4 royal
5 grande

a Anjou
b bouteille
c kir
d salade
e steak

WORTH KNOWING

In restaurants, you'll often find two or three set meals with *un menu gastronomique* (generally the top-priced set meal with specialities of the region) and perhaps *un menu pour enfants* (special set meal for children). You'll also see displayed *le plat du jour* (the dish of the day). Some set meals will include the wine: *une carafe* or *un pichet* (jug) *de vin de pays* (local wine).

You'll find a wide range of eating places. If you fancy a quick meal, try *la brasserie, le snack-bar, le drugstore* or *le fast-food*. For something different, go to *une crêperie* where you'll be able to taste delicious *galettes* (savoury pancakes) and *crêpes* (pancakes) with all sorts of fillings. Try *une galette au jambon et fromage* (with ham and cheese) *une galette aux champignons* (with mushrooms) or *une crêpe à la confiture d'abricot* (with apricot jam).

Here's a selection of some of the most common snacks:

le croque-monsieur	toasted sandwich with ham and cheese
le croque-madame	toasted sandwich with ham and cheese and an egg on top
le sandwich au jambon	ham sandwich
le sandwich au fromage	cheese sandwich
le sandwich au pâté	pâté sandwich
le sandwich aux rillettes	potted pork sandwich
le sandwich au saucisson	garlic sausage sandwich
le beignet	doughnut
le chausson aux pommes	apple turnover

This is a typical set meal:

Restaurant L'Escargot

Menu à 134,00 F

ENTRÉE AU CHOIX:	CHOICE OF STARTER:
terrine de pâté de canard	duck pâté terrine
ou	or
melon au porto	melon with port
ou	or
assiette de crudités	salad
PLAT PRINCIPAL AU CHOIX:	CHOICE OF MAIN DISH:
entrecôte grillée	grilled steak
ou	or
filet de porc normande	loin of pork Normandy
FROMAGE	CHEESE
DESSERTS	DESSERTS
Service 15% compris	*15% service included*

Finally, a few words on wine: You'll have heard of *vin blanc, vin rouge, vin rosé,* but have you heard of *vin jaune* and *vin de paille* (where the grapes are dried on straw before being pressed) from the Jura area? They're well worth tasting when you're next in that part of France. Wines vary from one region to another, from the fruity wines of Alsace to the dry white wines of the Loire valley. The wines of France fall into several categories:

- *vin ordinaire* is ordinary everyday table wine and normally a jolly good plonk!

- *vin de pays* has a higher ranking, in that it qualifies for departmental or local status, for example *vin de l'Ardèche*.
- *vins délimités de qualité supérieure* or *VDQS* are wines which are subject to regulations regarding the type of grapes used and the vinification.
- *Appellation d'origine contrôlée (AOC)* is the label under which the best wines are to be found.

To choose a good bottle of wine, you need to look carefully both at the label, and the year the wine was produced (known as the *millésime*).

6 DOWN TO BUSINESS

KEY WORDS AND PHRASES

je suis Monsieur Pierre Bouillon	I'm Mr Pierre Bouillon
Puis-je vous présenter mon collègue?	May I introduce my colleague to you?
j'ai rendez-vous avec Monsieur Doreau	I've an appointment with Monsieur Doreau
Quand pouvons-nous nous revoir?	When can we meet again?
Vous êtes libre lundi?	Are you free on Monday?
à quinze heures	at 3.00 pm
je crois qu'il est disponible	I think he's available
ah non, je regrette	oh no, I'm sorry
je voudrais parler à Monsieur Doreau	I'd like to speak to Monsieur Doreau
je rappellerai à partir de dix-sept heures	I'll call again after 5.00 p.m.
Quel est votre nom?	What's your name
Comment s'appellent-ils?	What are their names?
Vous habitez à Angers?	Do you live in Angers?
Vous êtes marié(e)?	Are you married?
Vous avez des enfants?	Have you got children?
Quel âge ont-ils?	How old are they?

CONVERSATIONS

ARRIVING FOR AN APPOINTMENT

M. BOUILLON	Bonjour, madame.
MME CELESTE	Bonjour, monsieur.
M. BOUILLON	Je suis Monsieur Pierre Bouillon de la société Cointreau. J'ai rendez-vous avec Monsieur Doreau à dix heures.
MME CELESTE	Oui. Asseyez-vous. Je vais le prévenir.
M. BOUILLON	Merci.
MME CELESTE	*(Going into Monsieur Doreau's office)* Monsieur Doreau, Monsieur Bouillon de la société Cointreau est arrivé.

MAY I INTRODUCE

M. BOUILLON	Puis-je vous présenter mon collègue, Monsieur Michaud.
M. DOREAU	Avec plaisir. Bonjour, Monsieur Michaud. Comment allez-vous?
M. MICHAUD	Bonjour, Monsieur Doreau. Très bien, merci.

ON THE TELEPHONE

MME CELESTE	Allô.
M. MICHAUD	Allô. Bonjour, madame. Je voudrais parler à Monsieur Doreau, s'il vous plaît.
MME CELESTE	Oui, monsieur. Mais Monsieur Doreau est en conférence.
M. MICHAUD	Quand est-ce que je peux le joindre?
MME CELESTE	A partir de cinq heures ce soir, monsieur.
M. MICHAUD	Bien, merci. Je rappellerai à partir de cinq heures. Au revoir, madame.
MME CELESTE	Au revoir, monsieur.

ARRANGING ANOTHER MEETING

M. BOUILLON Bien, Monsieur Michaud, quand pouvons-nous nous revoir?

M. MICHAUD Eh bien, pourquoi pas mercredi, quatorze heures?

M. BOUILLON Mercredi, quatorze heures . . .
Non, ce n'est pas possible. Est-ce possible jeudi à quinze heures?

M. MICHAUD Jeudi, quinze heures . . . tout a fait!

M. BOUILLON D'accord. Très bien.

I'D LIKE TO MEET . . . , TOO

M. BOUILLON Je voudrais aussi rencontrer Monsieur Larchet, jeudi après-midi.

M. MICHAUD Jeudi après-midi. Oui, je crois qu'il est disponible.

M. BOUILLON Très bien. C'est parfait.

ARRANGING TO MEET

M. JAMET Est-ce que vous êtes libre lundi à quinze heures?

MLLE COCHIN Ah non, je regrette, pas lundi à quinze heures.

M. JAMET Et jeudi à dix-huit heures?

MLLE COCHIN Dix-huit heures . . . c'est parfait, oui.

M. JAMET Entendu. Au revoir, mademoiselle.

MLLE COCHIN Au revoir, monsieur.

ARRIVING FOR AN APPOINTMENT

MARIE-PIERRE Pardon, monsieur. Monsieur Michaud.

M. MICHAUD Oui, tout à fait.

MARIE-PIERRE Marie-Pierre Méchineau, bonjour.

M. MICHAUD Ah, Marie-Pierre, bonjour. Nous avons rendez-vous, n'est-ce pas?

MARIE-PIERRE Oui, à neuf heures.

M. MICHAUD Bien. Entrez, s'il vous plaît.

HOW CAN I CONTACT YOU?

MARIE-PIERRE	Monsieur Michaud, vous pouvez me donner votre numéro de téléphone au bureau, s'il vous plaît?
M. MICHAUD	Oui. bien sûr. C'est le quarante et un.
MARIE-PIERRE	Oui.
M. MICHAUD	Trente-sept . . .
MARIE-PIERRE	Oui.
M. MICHAUD	Trente, zéro, zéro. Poste quarante-deux, quarante.
MARIE-PIERRE	D'accord, merci beaucoup. Et votre numéro de télex?
M. MICHAUD	Alors le télex, sept cent vingts, neuf cent quatre-vingt six.
MARIE-PIERRE	Bien. Vous avez un numéro de fax?
M. MICHAUD	Oui, bien sûr. C'est le quarante et un, quarante-trois, trente, quatorze.
MARIE-PIERRE	D'accord, merci beaucoup.

SOCIALISING

MARIE-PIERRE	Quel est votre nom?
M. BOUILLON	Pierre Bouillon.
MARIE-PIERRE	Vous êtes d'Angers?
M. BOUILLON	Non, je ne suis pas d'Angers.
MARIE-PIERRE	Vous êtes d'où?
M. BOUILLON	Je suis de Tours.
MARIE-PIERRE	Mais vous habitez à Angers maintenant?
M. BOUILLON	Oui, bien sûr.
MARIE-PIERRE	Et vous aimez?
M. BOUILLON	Oui, tout à fait.

ASKING ABOUT SOMEONE'S FAMILY

MARIE-PIERRE	Quel est votre nom?
MME LEBRETON	Marie-Noël Lebreton.
MARIE-PIERRE	Vous êtes mariée?
MME LEBRETON	Oui, je suis mariée.
MARIE-PIERRE	Et vous avez des enfants?
MME LEBRETON	Oui, j'en ai trois.
MARIE-PIERRE	Quel âge ont-ils?
MME LEBRETON	Dix ans, huit ans et quatre ans.
MARIE-PIERRE	Et comment s'appellent-ils?
MME LEBRETON	François, Marie et Alice.
MARIE-PIERRE	Oh, c'est joli!

WORD LIST

la société	company
asseyez-vous	do sit down
je vais le prévenir	I'll let him know
. . . est arrivé	. . . has arrived
allô	hello (on the phone)
en conférence	in a meeting
Pourquoi pas?	Why not?
tout à fait	absolutely
aussi	also
rencontrer	meet
entendu!	fine!
après-midi	afternoon
nous avions	we had
numéro de télex/fax	telex/fax number
Vous aimez (Angers)?	Do you like (Angers)?
joli(e)	pretty

EXPLANATIONS

BUSINESS INTRODUCTIONS

To introduce yourself, and say which company you work for:
Je suis Pierre Bouillon, de la société Cointreau
Je m'appelle Marie-Noël Lebreton, de la société Thompson
Je suis John Bell de la société Turbo

To introduce someone else:
Puis-je vous présenter mon collègue, Monsieur Michaud
Voici Marie-Pierre

Puis-je . . . ? is the equivalent of 'may I . . . ?'

APPOINTMENTS

To say you have an appointment:
J'ai rendez-vous avec Monsieur Doreau à dix heures

To find out when someone is free/available:
Vous êtes libre lundi à quinze heures?
Vous êtes disponible jeudi à neuf heures?

You can also say:
Quand pouvons-nous nous revoir? When can we meet again?

ON THE TELEPHONE

I'd like/May I speak to . . . (*on the telephone*)
Je voudrais parler à Monsieur Doreau
Puis-je parler à Monsieur Michaud?

To find out when you can get in touch with someone:
Quand est-ce que je peux le joindre? (him)
Quand est-ce que je peux la contacter? (her)

To say when you'll call again:
Je rappellerai à partir de cinq heures

When you give a French telephone or fax number to someone you have to break the number into pairs:
C'est le quarante-et-un, trente-sept, trente, zéro, zéro
Notice that 00 is *zéro zéro* and that 07 is *zéro sept*.

TALKING ABOUT FAMILIES

If asked how many children you have, say, for example:
J'en ai trois
En means 'of them' in sentences like:

Vous aves des enfants? { *Oui, j'en ai trois* / *Oui, j'en ai un* / *Non, je n'en ai pas*

It can also mean 'some' or 'any':
Vous avez du pain? *Oui, j'en ai*
Vous voulez de l'eau *Non, je n'en veux pas*

How old are they? What are their names?
Quel âge ont-ils?
Comment s'appellent-ils?

Instead of repeating the noun les enfants, Marie-Pierre used *ils* meaning 'they'.
If the noun is masculine, use *il:*
Je voudrais rencontrer Monsieur Larchet
Oui, je crois qu'il est disponible

If it's a feminine, use *elle:*
Est-ce que Mademoiselle Cochin est libre?
Non elle est au téléphone

If 'they' refers to a plural feminine noun, use *elles*
J'ai deux filles (daughters); *elles s'appellent Maude et Gabrielle*

VERBS

When you're talking with other people, you'll obviously use you (*vous*) and I (*je*) a lot. Remember that in French the verb ending changes much more often than in English.

With *vous*, almost all verbs end with *-ez:*

Vous habitez à Angers?	Do you live in Angers?
Vous avez des enfants?	Do you have any children?
Vous voulez un apéritif?	Would you like an aperitif?

But one very common exception:

Vous êtes d'Angers?	Are you from Angers?

With *je*, the endings are more varied:

Je regrette	I'm sorry (*formal*)
Je vous remercie	Thank you (*formal*)
Je crois qu'il est disponible	I think he's free
Je vous dois combien?	How much do I owe you?
Je vais prendre le menu à soixante	I'll have the set meal at 60,00 F
J'ai un rendez-vous avec Monsieur Doreau	I've a meeting with Monsieur Doreau
Je suis de Tours	I'm from Tours
Je peux vous payer?	Can I pay you?

EXERCISES

1 BUSINESS INTRODUCTIONS

a Introduce yourself.

b Say you have an appointment at 10.30 a.m. with Monsieur Doreau.

c Introduce your colleague, Madame Méchineau to Monsieur Doreau.

d You have to arrange another meeting with Monsieur Doreau. Ask him when he's free.

e When he suggests a time, say you're sorry, you're not available.

2 SOCIALISING

How would each of the people below answer these questions?:

Quel est votre nom?
Vous êtes d'où?
Vous êtes marié(e)?
Vous avez des enfants?
Quel âge ont-ils?
Comment s'appellent-ils?

a Peter Brown from London, married with two children, Mary (10) and Phillip (12)
b Jane Roberts from New York, married with three children, Simon (16), James (19) and Sally (22)
c Pierre Benoît from Reims, married with no children

3 NUMBERS

What are the following telephone and fax numbers in French?

a tél 41 32 78 00

____

b fax 41 78 61 67

____

c tél 44 56 78 09

____

d fax 44 54 12 60

____

e tél 010 33 70 57 64 15

____

f fax 010 33 70 24 67 89

____

4 ANSWERS USING '*EN*'

Answer these questions, using *en* in each answer:

a Vous avez des enfants? *Yes, three.*
b Vous avez un rendez-vous ce soir? *Yes, two.*
c Combien de tranches de saucisson voulez-vous? *I'd like ten.*
d Vous avez une voiture? *Yes, one.*
e Vous avez des chambres de libre? *No, I haven't.*

5 WHAT'S MISSING?

Fill in the blanks:

VOUS	Allô, Je . . . . Sophie Thireau de la . . . . Turbo. Je . . . . parler . . . . Monsieur Fichu, s'il vous plaît.
MME CELESTE	Je . . . . madame. Monsieur Fichu est absent.
VOUS	Quand puis-je le . . . . ?
MME CELESTE	Ce soir, ... de dix-neuf heures.
VOUS	D'accord. . . . . beaucoup. madame. Je . . . à dix-neuf heures.

WORTH KNOWING

The French telephone network is divided into *Paris* (and its suburbs) and *la province* (the rest of France). All subscribers have an eight-figure number. To make a telephone call within France, you have three possibilities:

- within Paris or la province, dial the eight-figure number only
- from Paris to la province, dial 16, wait for the tone *(la tonalité)*, then dial the eight-figure number
- from la province to Paris, dial 16, wait for the tone, then dial 1, followed by the eight-figure number

To telephone Great Britain from France, dial 19 and wait for the tone, then 44 followed by the British area code (omitting the '0' at the start) and the number you want to contact.

Here are a few useful telephone expressions:

Qui est à l'appareil?	Who's speaking?
Monsieur Bouillon à l'appareil	Monsieur Bouillon speaking

Veuillez patienter / *Conservez* / *Ne quittez pas* }	hold the line
Poste quarante-deux	Extension 42
Vous pouvez me passer Marie-Pierre?	Can you put me through to Marie-Pierre?

It may be useful to know what your job is in French, or to be able to say what sort of work you do. Here are a few tips to help:

le président directeur général chairman
la secrétaire de direction personal assistant
le/la comptable accountant
le chef du personnel personnel manager
le cadre executive
l'ingénieur (m) engineer
le directeur des ventes sales manager
le banquier banker
le chef du service export export manager
l'infirmière/infirmier female nurse/male nurse
le contremaître foreman
le boulanger/la boulangère baker
l'hôtesse de l'air (f) air hostess

Je travaille dans l'industrie automobile
I work in the car industry
Je travaille à la Chambre de Commerce
I work at the Chamber of Commerce
Je travaille dans l'agro-alimentaire
I work in the food industry
Je travaille chez Cointreau
I work at Cointreau's
Je suis à la retraite/retraité
I'm retired

CAN YOU GET BY?

Try these questions when you've finished the course. The answers are on page 88–9.

1 MEETING PEOPLE AND ORDERING DRINKS

a How do you greet people in the evening?
b How do you say: 'How are you?'
c How do you say: 'Where are you from?'
d Say 'please' and 'thank you' (give two answers).
e Say to the waiter: 'For me, an orange juice'.

2 SHOPPING

a Ask the stallholder: 'Do you have any apples?'
b Say you'd like three kilos of oranges.
c Ask how much it is.
d Tell the petrol pump attendant: 'Fill it up with unleaded 4-star'.
e Ask for 12 stamps at the post-office.

3 GETTING ABOUT

a Say: 'First street on the right, second on the left and then straight on'.
b Ask: 'Is there a petrol station nearby?'
c Stop a passer-by and ask what the time is.
d Say: 'I'd like a return ticket to Bordeaux'.
e Somebody is speaking too fast. Say: 'I'm sorry but I don't understand. Slowly, please'.

4 FINDING SOMEWHERE TO STAY

a Ask Monsieur Ocher whether there's a room available.
b Say you have a reservation for three nights, from 3 June till 6 June.
c Say you'd like a room with a double bed and shower.
d Ask what time breakfast is served.
e Ask for your key at the hotel reception (key number is 215).

5 EATING OUT

a Tell Monsieur Veger you'd like two set meals at 97,00 F and one at 125,00 F.
b Ask for a bottle of white wine and a bottle of mineral water.
c At the pâtisserie, say you'd like a pastry with chocolate in the middle and a lemon tea.
d Ask for two black coffees and a white one.
e Say: 'I'd like the bill, please'.

6 DOWN TO BUSINESS

a Introduce yourself: name, age, marital status, number of children.
b Ask Monsieur Doreau whether he's free on Thursday.
c Say you've an appointment with Monsieur Doreau at 4.00 p.m.
d Ask Monsieur Doreau whether he has a fax number.
e His number is 45 31 92 11. What does he tell you?

REFERENCE SECTION

PRONUNCIATION GUIDE

Coping with the sounds of a foreign language seems daunting at first. With time and practice, however, you'll soon manage to make yourself understood quite easily. Just listen carefully to what is being said and don't be disheartened if you cannot always make yourself understood first time. This is only a rough guide to pronunciation, but it will help you cope.

VOWELS

a1 short as in 'apple' or 'lack'
addition, salade

a2 long as in 'car'
âge, pâtisserie

e1 is generally similar to 'a' as in 'about'
le, de, petit

e2 is similar to 'e' as in 'let'
merci, essence, escargot
at the end of words like *douche, grande, petite, e* is not pronounced
in words ending in *-er* and *ez,* for example *aller, prenez,* it's pronounced like *é*

é is similar to a shortened 'ay' as in 'day'
marié, entrée

è/ê is similar to *e2*
collègue, crème, vous êtes

i is similar to 'i' in police
kilo, frites, tant pis

o can be short as in 'odd'
société, cognac

o at the end of a word, or *ô,* is long, similar to 'o' as in 'post'
numéro, hôtel

oi is pronounced 'wa'
droite, bonsoir

ou is pronounced 'oo'
vous, bonjour

u is similar to 'ew' as in 'threw'
rue, super, une

NASALS

These are vowel sounds followed by an 'n'. Listen carefully to the examples on the casette.

1 *-in* *vin*
-un *un steak, un plan de la ville*
-ain *pain*
-ien *bien, combien*
-ein *le plein*

2 *-en* *entrez*
-an *blanc*

3 *-on* *bon*

CONSONANTS

A consonant at the end of a word is often not pronounced: *vous voulez, petit, grand, anglais.* But there are some exceptions, for example, *cognac.*

The following consonants sound much the same in French and in English:

b; d; f; k; l; m; n; p; s; t; v; z

The following are slightly different:

c + *a, o, u* or a consonant is like 'c' in 'cot'
café, cointreau

c + *e* or *i* is like 's' in 'signal'
celui-ci, merci, Béatrice

ç is like 's' in 'signal'
ça va, française

ch is like 'sh' in 'ship'
château, marché

g + *a, o, u* or a consonant is like 'g' as in 'gap'
gauche, baguette, grand

gn is like 'n' in 'onion'
champagne

h is usually not pronounced
hôtel, heure

j is like 's' in 'pleasure'
je, Anjou

ph is like the English 'f'
pharmacie

qu is like 'k' in 'kilo'
quatre, quelle heure

r comes from the back of the mouth. Listen carefully to the examples on the tape
bière, restaurant, kir royal

t followed by *-ion* is pronounced 's'
station d'essence, réservation

th is like 't' in 'table'
thé

NUMBERS

0	*zéro*
1	*un/une*
2	*deux*
3	*trois*
4	*quatre*
5	*cinq*
6	*six*
7	*sept*
8	*huit*
9	*neuf*
10	*dix*
11	*onze*
12	*douze*
13	*treize*
14	*quatorze*
15	*quinze*
16	*seize*
17	*dix-sept*
18	*dix-huit*
19	*dix-neuf*
20	*vingt*
21	*vingt et un*
22	*vingt-deux*
23	*vingt-trois*
30	*trente*
40	*quarante*
50	*cinquante*
60	*soixante*
70	*soixante-dix*
71	*soixante et onze*
72	*soixante-douze*
80	*quatre-vingts*
81	*quatre-vingt-un*
90	*quatre-vingt-dix*
91	*quatre-vingt-onze*
100	*cent*
101	*cent un*
102	*cent deux*
200	*deux cents*
201	*deux cent un*
300	*trois cents*
1000	*mille*

FIRST, SECOND, THIRD

1st	*premier/première*
2nd	*deuxième*
3rd	*troisième*
9th	*neuvième*
11th	*onzième*
21st	*vingt et unième*

DAYS OF THE WEEK

lundi	Monday
mardi	Tuesday
mercredi	Wednesday
jeudi	Thursday
vendredi	Friday
samedi	Saturday
dimanche	Sunday

MONTHS OF THE YEAR

janvier	January
février	February
mars	March
avril	April
mai	May
juin	June
juillet	July
août	August
septembre	September
octobre	October
novembre	November
décembre	December

KEY TO THE EXERCISES

1 MEETING PEOPLE AND ORDERING DRINKS

1 GREETINGS

a Bonjour, Marie-Pierre. Comment allez-vous?/ (Comment) ça va?
b Bonsoir, Anne.
c Bonjour, Monsieur Bouillon. Comment allez-vous?
d Au revoir Monsieur Doreau.
e Bonjour, madame.

2 AT THE 'CAFE'

S'il vous plaît
Deux bières, s'il vous plaît
Pression, s'il vous plaît

3 NUMBERS

a trois • cinq • sept • huit • dix
b dix • cinq • six • neuf • dix

4 ORDERING DRINKS

a Un thé au citron, s'il vous plaît.
b Deux cafés, s'il vous plaît.
c Trois jus d'orange, s'il vous plaît.
d Un cointreau, s'il vous plaît.

5 MIX AND MATCH

1c • 2d • 3b • 4e • 5a

2 SHOPPING

1 HERE'S YOUR SHOPPING LIST

J'aimerais . . . *or* Je voudrais . . . s'il vous plaît.

a une bouteille de vin rouge
b trois baguettes
c quatre cent cinquante grammes de gruyère
d huit tranches de saucisson (à l'ail)
e deux kilos de pommes
f une livre de tomates

2 MIXED UP

b • a • e • d • c

– Qu'est-ce que vous voulez?
– 450 grammes de gruyère, s'il vous plaît.
– Et avec ceci?
– Du saucisson.
– Combien de tranches?
– Huit tranches de saucisson.
– Vous voulez autre chose?
– Des pommes.
– Combien de kilos?
– Deux kilos de pommes.

3 HOW MUCH?

a 25,60 F • **b** 2,80 F • **c** 14,33 F • **d** quinze francs • **e** neuf francs cinquante • **f** treize francs vingt-neuf

4 AT THE FRUIT MARKET

– Bonjour, mademoiselle.
– Un kilo de pommes.
– Six tomates, s'il vous plaît.
– Merci. C'est combien les oranges?

5 A FEW NECESSITIES!

a Je voudrais un guide d'Angers, s'il vous plaît.
b Je voudrais changer deux cents livres sterling en francs français.
c Je voudrais quatre timbres pour la Grande-Bretagne.
d Je voudrais vingt litres d'essence sans plomb.

3 OUT AND ABOUT

1 DIRECTIONS

a Vous prenez la Rue Toussaint. Vous continuez tout droit et le château est devant vous.
b Vous prenez/montez (*go up*) le Boulevard du Roi René sur votre gauche et vous allez jusqu'aux feux (*traffic lights*). Puis vous tournez à gauche. Vous prenez le Boulevard du Maréchal Foch. Vous continuez tout droit et le Jardin du Mail est sur votre droite.
c Vous prenez/descendez (*go down*) la Rue St Aubin. Au bout de la Rue St Aubin, vous tournez à gauche. Puis vous prenez la Rue Toussaint. Vous continuez tout droit. Le musée est sur votre gauche.

2 WHAT TIME IS IT?

a dix heures vingt-cinq (du matin)
b une heure quarante (de l'après-midi) or treize heures quarante
c quatre heures cinq (du matin)
d neuf heures trente (du soir) or vingt et une heures trente
e quinze heures dix
f treize heures quinze
g vingt et une heures trente-cinq
h zéro heure quarante-deux

3 HOW DO I GET TO . . . ?

- Excusez-moi/Pardon.
- Pour aller au château, s'il vous plaît?
- Pardon. Plus lentement, s'il vous plaît.
- A gauche . . . le boulevard du Roi René.
- D'accord. Et c'est loin?
- D'accord/Bien. Merci beaucoup/Je vous remercie beaucoup.
- Au revoir.

4 BOOKING TRAIN TICKETS

a Un aller-retour pour Lyon, en seconde.
b Deux allers simples pour Lille, en première.
c Un aller simple pour Marseille, en seconde.
d Il y a un train pour Saumur à dix heures?
e C'est quel quai?
f C'est combien un aller-retour en première?

5 OPENING AND CLOSING TIMES

a The museum is open from 10.00 until 17.30 every day except Sunday when it is closed.
b The castle is open from 9.30 until 18.00; closed on Mondays.
c The cathedral is open betwen 9.00 and 18.00 every day.

4 FINDING SOMEWHERE TO STAY

1 BOOKING HOTEL ROOMS

a Vous avez deux chambres avec/à un grand lit, avec bain, pour trois nuits?
b Vous avez une chambre à deux lits, avec douche, pour cette nuit?
c Je voudrais réserver une chambre à un lit, avec cabinet de toilette, du 9 au 12 août.

d Je voudrais réserver une chambre à un grand lit et un lit d'enfant, avec douche, pour la semaine prochaine.

e Vous avez une chambre avec douche pour un enfant et une chambre avec bain pour deux adultes?

2 MIX AND MATCH

1c • 2d • 3a • 4b

3 SPEAKING TO THE RECEPTIONIST

a Vous avez des chambres de libre, s'il vous plaît?
b C'est combien la chambre avec cabinet de toilette?
c (Est-ce que) le petit déjeuner est compris?
d A quelle heure est-ce que vous servez le petit déjeuner?

4 THERE MUST BE SOME MISTAKE!

– Bonsoir.
– J'ai une réservation pour une chambre à un grand lit, avec douche.
– Je m'appelle Stuart.
– Je ne comprends pas.
– (Est-ce qu')il y a un autre hôtel près d'ici?
– Merci.

5 FILL THE GAPS

Nom: Paine
Prénom: Liz
Numéro du passeport: 934507 D
Numéro d'immatriculation du véhicule: H 789 ABC
Nombre de personnes: *adultes:* deux
enfants: trois

Caravane: oui
Tente: oui
Electricité: oui
Nombre de nuits: sept
Dates: du vingt-trois au vingt-neuf juillet

5 EATING OUT

1 WHICH WOULD YOU CHOOSE?

1c • 2a • 3c • 4c • 5a

2 WHAT DID THEY ORDER?

Apéritif Marie-Pierre: un kir royal • Pierrick: un whisky • Marc: un ricard
Entrée Marie-Pierre, Pierrick et Marc: les escargots
Plat principal Pierrick et Marc: un filet mignon • Marie-Pierre: une sole meunière
Vins avec les escargots, un Anjou blanc, puis un Chinon
Dessert Marie-Pierre et Marc: une Fôret-Noire au chocolat • Pierrick: une pêche melba
Café Marie-Pierre et Marc: un café
Digestif Pierrick: un petit cognac • Marc: un cointreau

3 IN A RESTAURANT

a Une table pour trois, s'il vous plaît.
b Un menu à soixante-quinze (francs) et deux à cent quarante (francs).
c Un martini, un whisky et un kir pour moi.
d Un steak saignant et un steak à point *or* Deux steaks, un saignant et l'autre à point, et une sole meunière.
e Une bouteille d'Anjou blanc.
f Trois pêches melba.
g Deux cafés et un crème.
h L'addition s'il vous plaît.

4 FILL THE GAPS

a au **b** à la **c** au **d** à la **e** au **f** à l' **g** à la

5 MIXED UP!

l • b • i • k • g • e • a • c • f • j • d • h

6 MIX AND MATCH

1d • 2a • 3e • 4c • 5b

6 DOWN TO BUSINESS

BUSINESS INTRODUCTIONS

a Je m'appelle or je suis Madame/Mademoiselle/ Monsieur . . .

b J'ai un rendez-vous à dix heures trente avec Monsieur Doreau.

c Voici ma collègue Madame Méchineau.

d Quand est-ce que vous êtes libre?/Quand êtes-vous libre?/ Vous êtes libre quand?

e Je suis désolé. Je ne suis pas libre.

2 SOCIALISING

a Je m'appelle Peter Brown. Je suis de Londres. Je suis marié et j'ai deux enfants, Mary dix ans et Philip douze ans.

b Je m'appelle Jane Roberts. Je suis de New York. Je suis mariée et j'ai trois enfants, Simon seize ans, James dix-neuf ans et Sally vingt-deux ans.

c Je m'appelle Pierre Benoît. Je suis de Reims. Je suis marié mais je n'ai pas d'enfants.

3 NUMBERS

a quarante et un; trente-deux; soixante-dix-huit; zéro zéro

b quarante et un; soixante-dix-huit; soixante et un; soixante-sept

c quarante-quatre; cinquante-six; soixante-dix-huit; zéro neuf

d quarante-quatre; cinquante-quatre; douze; soixante

e zéro dix; trente-trois; soixante-dix; cinquante-sept; soixante-quatre; quinze

f zéro dix; trente-trois; soixante-dix; vingt-quatre; soixante-sept; quatre-vingt-neuf

4 ANSWERS USING '*EN*'

a J'en ai trois.
b J'en ai deux.
c J'en voudrais dix.
d J'en ai une.
e Je n'en ai pas.

5 WHAT'S MISSING?

VOUS	m'appelle • société • voudrais • à
MME CELESTE	suis désolée
VOUS	contacter
MME CELESTE	à partir de
VOUS	merci • rappellerai

CAN YOU GET BY?

1 MEETING PEOPLE AND ORDERING DRINKS

a Bonsoir, madame/mademoiselle/monsieur.
b Comment allez-vous?/Ça va?
c Vous êtes d'où?
d S'il vous plaît • Merci/Je vous remercie.
e Pour moi, un jus d'orange.

2 SHOPPING

a Vous avez des pommes?
b Je voudrais trois kilos d'oranges.
c C'est combien?
d Le plein de super sans plomb.
e Je voudrais douze timbres pour la Grande-Bretagne.

3 OUT AND ABOUT

a La première rue à droite, la deuxième à gauche et (c'est) tout droit.

b Il y a une station d'essence/une station-service près d'ici?
c Excusez-moi madame/monsieur. Quelle heure est-il/il est?
d Je voudrais un aller-retour pour Bordeaux.
e Je suis désolé, mais je ne comprends pas. Lentement, s'il vous plaît.

4 FINDING SOMEWHERE TO STAY

a Vous avez des chambres de libre?
b J'ai une réservation pour trois nuits (à partir) du 3 (jusqu') au 6 juin.
c J'aimerais une chambre à un grand lit, avec douche.
d Vous servez le petit déjeuner à quelle heure?/à quelle heure est-ce que vous servez le petit déjeuner?
e Je voudrais la clef numéro deux cent quinze.

5 EATING OUT

a Deux menus à quatre-vingt-dix-sept et un à cent vingt-cinq.
b (J'aimerais) une bouteille de vin blanc et une bouteille d'eau minérale.
c J'aimerais/Je voudrais un pain au chocolat et un thé au citron.
d Deux cafés et un crème, s'il vous plaît.
e L'addition, s'il vous plaît.

6 DOWN TO BUSINESS

a Je m'appelle . . . . J'ai . . . ans. Je suis marié(e)/Je ne suis pas marié(e)/Je suis célibataire (*single*). J'ai . . . enfants/Je n'ai pas d'enfants.
b Vous êtes libre jeudi?
c J'ai un rendez-vous avec Monsieur Doreau à quatre heures de l'après-midi/seize heures.
d Vous avez un numéro de fax?
e Le quarante-cinq trente et un quatre-vingt douze onze.

WORD LIST

A

d'accord fine/OK
l'addition (f) bill
l'adulte (m/f) adult
l'agneau (m) lamb
vous aimez . . . ? do you like . . . ?
aller to go
allez! go on!
l'aller-retour (m) return
l'aller simple (m) single
l'allumette (f) match
alors then
anglais(e) English
je m'appelle my name is
l'après-midi (m/f) afternoon
l'arrivée arrival
vous arrivez you arrive
l'asperge (f) asparagus
asseyez-vous sit down
au revoir goodbye/good night
autre chose (f) something else
nous avions we had

B

les bagages (m) luggage
la baguette French stick
le bain bath
la banque bank
le beurre butter
la bière beer
bien sûr of course
blanc white
boire to drink
la boîte box
bonjour (m) good morning
bonsoir (m) good evening/good night
la boulangerie baker's
la bouteille bottle
au bureau at the office/at work
le bureau de tabac tobacconist's

C

ça va? how are you?
ça va I'm fine
ça ne fait rien it does not matter
le cabinet de toilette washing facilities
le café coffee
le car coach
la caravane caravan
la carotte carrot
la carte postale postcard
la cathédrale cathedral
ceci this
avec ceci with this
cela that
cela vous fait . . . that will be . . .
celui-ci this one
celui-là that one
le centre-ville town centre
la cerise cherry
certainement certainly
la chambre room
changer to change
le château castle
chaud(e) hot/warm
le chocolat chocolate
vous avez choisi? have you chosen?
le cinquante et un aniseed based aperitif
le citron lemon
le citron pressé squeezed lemon juice
la clef key
le/la collègue colleague
combien how much/many
c'est combien? how much is it?
je vous dois combien? how much do I owe you?
comme as
comment how
comment allez-vous? how are you?
comment s'appellent-ils? what are their names?
complet/complète full
comprise included
compter to count
le concombre cucumber
en conférence (f) in a meeting
la crème de cassis blackcurrant liqueur
la crème de mûre blackberry liqueur
la crème de pêche peach liqueur

je crois I believe
cru(e) cured, raw
cuit(e) cooked

D

dans in
le départ departure
derrière behind
vous désirez? would you like?
désolé(e) sorry
deuxième second
le digestif liqueur
disponible available
donner to give
la douche shower
la douzaine dozen
droite right

E

l'eau water
également also
l'électricité (f) electricity
l'emplacement (m) place (at campsite)
encore once again
les enfants (m) children
entendu! fine!
l'entrée (f) starter
entrez come in
environ about
envoyer to send
épais(se) thick
les épinards (m) spinach
les escargots (m) snails
l'étage floor
l'essence (f) petrol/2-star petrol
vous êtes you are
excusez-moi excuse me
l'express (m) espresso (coffee)

F

facile easy
faire to do
fermer to close
le filet mignon pork fillet
fin(e) fine
les flageolets (m) dwarf kidney beans
la Fôret-Noire black forest gâteau
la fraise strawberry
français(e) French
froid(e) cold
le fromage cheese

G

la gare station
la gare routière coach station
gauche left
le guide guide
grand(e) big
la Grande-Bretagne Great Britain
gratuit(e) free

H

l'heure (f) time, hour
les haricots verts (m) green beans
l'horaire (m) timetable

I

ici here
il y a there is/are
inscrit booked

J

le jambon ham
joindre to get hold of
joli(e) pretty
le jus d'orange orange juice
jusqu'à till/up to

K

le kir white wine with blackcurrant liqueur
le kir royal champagne (or sparkling wine) with blackcurrant liqueur

L

là there
là-bas over there
le lait milk
les légumes (m) vegetables
lentement slowly
libre available/free
le lit bed
à un grand lit with a double bed
la livre 1lb (half a kilo); a pound (sterling)
loin far

M

maintenant now
malheureusement unfortunately
le marché market
marié(e) married
le menu set meal
merci (beaucoup/bien) thank you (very much)
moi me
pour me for me
moyen(ne) average
le musée museum

N

le nom name
la note bill
la nuit night
le numéro number

O

l'œuf (m) egg
où where
d'où from where
ouvert(e) open

P

le pain bread
le pain au chocolat pastry with chocolate in the middle
le pain aux raisins pastry with currants
pardon excuse me
parfait(e) perfect
le parfum flavour
le parking car park
partir to leave
le passeport passport
les pâtisseries (f) cakes and pastries
payer to pay
la pêche peach
la pêche melba peach melba
la personne person
petit(e) small
le petit déjeuner breakfast
je peux . . . ? can I . . . ?
la pharmacie chemist's
à pied on foot
la place space, square (in a town)
avec plaisir with pleasure
s'il vous plaît please
le plan map
le plat dish
le plein (d'essence) fill it up
à point medium (steak)
la pomme apple
la pomme de terre potato
les pommes frites (f) chips
le porto port
le poste extension
pourquoi why
premier/première first
première classe first class
prendre to take
vous prenez? are you taking?
préparer to prepare
près near
tout près d'ici very near here
la pression draught beer
prévenir to let somebody know
je vous en prie my pleasure
prochain(e) next
puis-je . . . ? may I . . . ?

Q

le quai platform
quand when
quel(le) what
quelle heure est-il? what time is it?
à quelle heure ferme . . . ? what time does . . . close?
quel âge ont-ils? how old are they?

R

je rappellerai I'll call again
regarder to look
je regrette I'm sorry
je vous remercie thank you
rencontrer to meet
le rendez-vous appointment
réserver to book
revoir to meet again
rien du tout nothing at all
la rue street
la rue piétonne pedestrian street

S

saignant(e) rare (steak)
la salade verte lettuce
la salle de bains bathroom
le saucisson (à l'ail) (garlic) sausage
en seconde (classe) in second class
la semaine week
ce sera tout that will be all
je vous sers I'll serve you
vous servez you serve
la société company
le soir evening/night
ce soir tonight
la sole meunière sole fried in butter with lemon and parsley
nous sommes we are
la spécialité speciality
la station d'essence petrol station
je suis I am
vous suivez you follow
le super 4-star petrol
le super sans plomb 4-star unleaded
en supplément extra

T

tant pis never mind
tchin cheers
le *téléphérique* cable car
la *tente* tent
tenez here you are
le *thé* tea
le *thé nature* tea on its own
le *timbre* stamps
la *tomate* tomato
tous les jours everyday
tout à fait absolutely
tout de suite right away
tout droit straight ahead
la *tranche* slice
vous *traversez* you cross
très bien very well
la *truite* trout

V

vas-y go on
la *viande* meat
la *viennoiserie* viennese pastry
la *ville* town
le *vin* wine
voici here it is/you are
voilà there it is/you are
la *voiture* car
votre your
à la *vôtre* cheers
je *voudrais* I'd like
vous *voulez . . . ?* do you want . . . ?
voyons let's see